RETHINKING
―― *The* ――
RAPTURE

Stanford E. Murrell

Copyright © 2021 by Stanford E. Murrell

All rights reserved. No part of this publication may be reproduced, stored in a retrieval system, or transmitted, in any form or by any means, electronic, mechanical, photocopying, recording or otherwise, without prior permission of the publisher or the Copyright Licensing Agency.

Our goal is to provide high-quality, thought-provoking books that foster encouragement and spiritual growth. For more information regarding bulk purchases, other IP books, or our publishing services, visit us online or write to support@ichthuspublications.com.

Unless otherwise indicated, all Scripture quotations taken from the King James Version.

Cover images licensed by Shutterstock.

Printed in the United States of America.

ISBN: 978-1946971739

www.ichthuspublications.com

Contents

Section I: Where It All Began

Preface   The Tragic Tale of Margaret McDonald | 1

Section II: The Rapture in History

1   William Miller and the End of the World | 13
2   Are We in the Last Days? | 35
3   Why Do So Many People Believe in the Rapture? | 41
4   Inconsistency in the Rapture Theory | 53
5   Will the Bride of Christ be Raptured? | 57

Section III: The Rapture in Society

6   The Rapture in Schools | 67
7   The Rapture in the Cinema | 73
8   The Last Day of Human History | 81

Section IV: The Rapture in Doctrinal Review

9   Rapture Mania | 97
10   The System | 105
11   The Problem with the Rapture Theory | 111
12   The Resurrection and the Rapture: The Preterist View | 115

13	Being Caught Up	121
14	The Rapture Theory and *Harpazō*	125
15	The London Baptist Confession of Faith of 1689	131
16	Is the Rapture a Coming of Christ, Or Not?	137
17	What About Old Testament Rapture Types?	143
18	Personal Concerns with Classical Dispensationalism and the Rapture	149

"A lie told once remains a lie, but a lie told a thousand times becomes the truth."

—Joseph Goebbels

Section I:

Where It All Began

Preface

Like millions of other Christians, I was taught from childhood to believe in the doctrine of the Rapture, meaning that the Church is to be taken away from earth prior to a tumultuous seven-year period known as The Great Tribulation. The most well-known religious novel series, *Left Behind*, is based on this pretribulational rapture theory. Unfortunately, countless millions have been encouraged to believe the Rapture theory conveys a historical Christian faith, and biblical truth. Nothing could be more erroneous than that belief.

The idea of a pretribulational rapture is of recent origin, as author Dave MacPherson documents in his excellent work, *The Rapture Plot*. As MacPherson notes, the idea of a great escape from earth during a tribulation period is a concept that is not reflected in any of the major Creeds of Christendom. The Rapture was never discussed at any of the twenty-one ecumenical Church councils held over the centuries, and the dispensational view of the Rapture is certainly not found in the Bible, though Scripture is often alluded to.

My own objective in *Rethinking The Rapture* is to encourage God's people to return to Scripture and "Prove all things; hold fast that which is good" (1 Thess. 5:21). To that end, I encourage you to know something about a godly, but misguided young girl named Margaret MacDonald. Her tragic story is extracted in part from, *The Incredible Cover-up* by Dave MacPherson. Consider what MacPherson has written.

Margaret MacDonald was a young Scottish girl who is reported to have had a private revelation from God in Port Glasgow, Scotland, in the spring (March) of 1830. Margaret was born, January 14, 1815 and was baptized on January 22, 1815. She was 15 years old when she first had a revelation that had been hidden from all of God's people for nearly 2,000 years!

Margaret died on September 14, 1835 at the young age of 20, having lived a life full of Christian graces, all the while longing for more of the Spirit of God. For that, she is to be remembered, respected, and honored as an example of youthful faithfulness to Christ. In her unique revelation, Margaret came to understand that a select group of Christians would be caught up (raptured) to meet Christ in the air before the days of Antichrist. This was a novel revelation indeed.

A personal witness to her prophetic utterances was Robert Norton, M.D., who preserved her handwritten account of her pre-tribulation rapture revelation in two of his books and said it was the first time anyone had ever divided the Second Coming of Christ into two distinct parts or stages (*The Restoration of Apostles and Prophets; In the Catholic Apostolic Church; Memoirs of James and George Macdonald of Port-Glasgow*, 1840).

A New Teaching Spreads

Margaret's new revelations were well known to those who visited her home, among them John Darby of the Brethren. In the September 1830 issue of "The Morning Watch," the new revelations of Margaret were being presented. The early disciples of the pre-tribulation interpretation often called it a new doctrine. For example, one of the earliest Brethren leaders, Robert Gribble, confessed in the early 1830s that he had adopted "a new view of unfulfilled prophecy" (Harold H. Rowdon, *The Origins of the Brethren*, p. 149).

John Darby advocated a subtle introduction of the doctrine of the new pre-tribulation rapture view. "I think we ought to have something more of direct testimony as the Lord's coming, and its bearing also on the state of the Church: ordinarily, it would not be well to have it so clear, as it frightens people. We must pursue it steadily; it works like leaven, and its fruit is by no means seen yet; I do not mean leaven as ill, but the thoughts are new, and people's minds work on them, and all the old habits are against their feelings...." (*Letters of John N. Darby*, pp. 25–26).

The Setting of Dates

It is important to realize that this whole Rapture doctrine is new to Christian theology, as John Nelson Darby admitted. It is not just rediscovered truth in the manner of the Reformers. What was not new was the setting of dates. John Darby himself was a date setter at one time. In his *Etudes sur l'Epitre aux Hebreux*, published in Lausanne, Switzerland, about 1835, Darby writes,

"There are excellent brethren in all countries who have sought to calculate these dates... some have fixed 1844, others 1847; I myself have made several calculations in the times past, and in the same sense."

Pretribulation Rapture Doctrine of Margaret MacDonald

The following is the story of the revelation of Margaret MacDonald told in her own words:

> It was first the awful state of the land that was pressed upon me. I saw the blindness and infatuation of the people to be very great. I felt the cry of Liberty just to be the hiss of the serpent, to drown them in perdition. It was just "no God." I repeated the words, "Now there is distress of nations, with perplexity, the seas and the roaring, men's hearts failing them for fear—now look out for the sign of the Son of man."
>
> Here I was made to stop and cry out, "O, it is not known what the sign of the Son of man is; the people of God think they are waiting, but they know not what it is."
>
> I felt this needed to be revealed, and that there was great darkness and error about it; but suddenly what it was burst upon me with a glorious light. I saw it was just the Lord himself descending from Heaven with a shout, just the glorified man, even Jesus; but that all must, as Stephen was, be filled with the Holy Ghost, that they might look up, and see the brightness of the Father's glory.

I saw the error to be, that men think that it will be something seen by the natural eye; but' tis spiritual discernment that is needed, the eye of God in his people. Many passages were revealed, in a light in which I had not before seen them. I repeated,

"Now is the kingdom of Heaven like unto ten virgins, who went forth to meet the Bridegroom, five wise and five foolish; they that were foolish took their lamps, but took no oil with them; but they that were wise took oil in their vessels with their lamps. But be ye not unwise, but understanding what the will of the Lord is; and be not drunk with wine wherein is excess, but be filled with the Spirit."

This was the oil the wise virgins took in their vessels--this is the light to be kept burning—the light of God—that we may discern that which cometh not with observation to the natural eye. Only those who have the light of God within them will see the sign of his appearance.

No need to follow them who say, "see here, or see there, for his day shall be as the lightning to those in whom the living Christ is. 'Tis Christ in us that will lift us up—he is the light—'tis only those that are alive in him that will be caught up to meet him in the air." I saw that we must be in the Spirit, that we might see spiritual things. John was in the Spirit, when he saw a throne set in Heaven. —But I saw that the glory of the ministration of the Spirit had not been known.

I repeated frequently, but the spiritual temple must and shall be reared, and the fullness of Christ be poured into his body, and then shall we be caught up to meet him. Oh, none will be counted worthy of this calling but his body, which is the Church, and which must be a candlestick all of gold. I often said, Oh, the glorious inbreaking of God which is now about to burst on this earth; Oh, the glorious temple which is now about to be reared, the bride adorned for her husband; and Oh, what a holy, holy bride she must be, to be prepared for such a glorious bridegroom. I said, "Now shall the people of God have to do with realities—now shall the glorious mystery of God in our nature be known—now shall it be known what it is for man to be glorified."

I felt that the revelation of Jesus Christ had yet to be opened up—it is not knowledge about God that it contains, but it is an entering into God—I saw that there was a glorious breaking in of God to be.

I felt as Elijah, surrounded with chariots of fire.

I saw as it were, the spiritual temple reared, and the Head Stone brought forth with shoutings of grace, grace, unto it. It was a glorious light above the brightness of the sun, that shone round about me.

I felt that those who were filled with the Spirit could see spiritual things, and feel walking in the midst of them, while those who had not the Spirit could see nothing—so that two shall be in one bed, the one taken and the other left, because the one has the light of God within while the other cannot see the Kingdom of Heaven.

I saw the people of God in an awfully dangerous situation, surrounded by nets and entanglements, about to be tried, and many about to be deceived and fall.

Preface

Now [after this] will *the wicked* be revealed, with all power and signs and lying wonders, so that if it were possible the very elect will be deceived.

This is the fiery trial which is to try us. It will be for the purging and purifying of the real members of the body of Jesus; but oh, it will be a fiery trial. Every soul will be shaken to the very center. The enemy will try to shake in everything we have believed—but the trial of real faith will be found to honour and praise and glory. Nothing but what is of God will stand. The stony-ground hearers will be made manifest—the love of many will wax cold.

I frequently said that night, and often since, now shall the awful sight of a false Christ be seen on this earth, and nothing but the living Christ in us can detect this awful attempt of the enemy to deceive—for it is with all deceivableness of unrighteousness he will work—he will have a counterpart for every part of God's truth, and an imitation for every work of the Spirit. The Spirit must and will be poured out on the Church, that she may be purified and filled with God—and just in proportion as the Spirit of God works, so will he—when our Lord anoints men with power, so will he. This is particularly the nature of the trial, through which those are to pass who will be counted worthy to stand before the Son of man. There will be outward trial too, but 'tis principally temptation. It is brought on by the outpouring of the Spirit, and will just increase in proportion as the Spirit is poured out. The trial of the Church is from Antichrist. It is by being filled with the Spirit that we shall be kept.

I frequently said, "Oh be filled with the Spirit—have the light of God in you, that you may detect Satan—be full of eyes within—be clay in the hands of the potter—submit to be filled, filled with God. This will build the temple. It is not by might nor by power, but my Spirit, saith the Lord. This will fit us to enter into the marriage supper of the Lamb."

I saw it to be the will of God that all should be filled. But what hindered the real life of God from being received by his people, was their turning from Jesus, who is the way to the Father. They were not entering in by the door. For he is faithful who hath said, by me if any man enter in he shall find pasture. They were passing from the cross, through which every drop of the Spirit of God flows to us. All power that comes not through the blood of Christ is not of God.

When I say, they are looking from the cross, I feel that there is much in it—they turn from the blood of the Lamb, by which we overcome, and in which our robes are washed and made white. There are low views of God's holiness, and a ceasing to condemn sin in the flesh, and a looking from him who humbled himself, and made himself of no reputation. Oh! it is needed, much needed at present, a leading back to the cross.

I saw that night, and often since, that there will be an outpouring of the Spirit on the body, such as has not been, a baptism of fire, that all the dross may be put away. Oh, there must and will be such an indwelling of the living God as has not been—the servants of God sealed in their foreheads—great conformity to Jesus—his holy,

holy image seen in his people—just the bride made comely, by his comeliness put upon her. This is what we are at present made to pray much for, that speedily we may all be made ready to meet our Lord in the air—and it will be. Jesus wants his bride. His desire is toward us. He that shall come, will come, and will not tarry. Amen and Amen. Even so come Lord Jesus.

Margaret MacDonald believed that the catching up, or Rapture, would be seen only by believers filled with the Spirit. This would be a secret coming. When she spoke of "one taken and the other left," it was not a separation of believers and unbelievers, but rather of Spirit-filled believers being taken, while non-Spirit believers are left to endure tribulation.

The major point to recognize is that Margaret believed some Christians are to be taken in a Rapture before the "Wicked One," or "Antichrist" is revealed.

With this information in mind, I encourage you to *rethink the rapture*. May the Lord bless your studies as you open His Word in order to be able to "earnestly contend for the faith, which was once delivered unto the saints" (Jude 3).

Stanford E. Murrell

Section II:

The Rapture in History

Chapter 1

William Miller and the End of the World

With hostilities raging in the Middle East, China on the move to dominate the globe, and Russia vying to reestablish historic borders of a former empire, interest in prophetic matters is heightened. To help guide Christian thoughts in the area of eschatology (the study of end times), it is good to remember the past in order not to misunderstand the present.

There are two passages of Scripture that have bearing on our subject. I invite you to turn in a Bible to the first, which is found in Matthew 25:6, "And at midnight there was a cry made, Behold, the bridegroom cometh; go ye out to meet him." The second passage is Habakkuk 2:3, "For the vision is yet for an appointed time, but at the end it shall speak, and not lie: though it tarry, wait for it; because it will surely come, it will not tarry."

With these biblical passages in mind, I want to tell you a story about a religious individual who made a bold prediction in the middle of the nineteenth century. Here is his story.

On the 22nd of October, 1844, people sat, or stood on a ledge in a place called Low Hampton, New York. Nearby, in a lovely white framed farmhouse, a 62-year-old Baptist itinerant preacher sat reading a Bible and praying. These people, and thousands more, from Portland, Maine to Boston, Massachusetts to New York, were called Millerites, which means they were disciples of the Baptist layman, William Miller. Many had sold or had given away all of their possessions in the preceding days. Some had even left unharvested crop in their fields. After all, they reasoned, it was useless to continue the labors and toil of this world—especially given the fact about what was about to take place. These pious followers had eaten what they thought was their last meal on earth. They, and William Miller, the man in the farmhouse, were waiting quietly and eagerly for the second advent of Christ—and the end of the world. It is difficult to calculate how many people believed, hoped, or feared that the world would end on that night, but the number is quite staggering. Estimates range anywhere from 100,000 to more than a million people. That means one out of every seventeen Americans at that time believed the end of the world was imminent; one out of every seventeen Americans were tragically mislead and profoundly disappointed.

Millennium Expectations

When an inquiry is made into why so many people, in so many places, believed the world was coming to an end in October of 1844, the answer is this: there were millennium expectations. These millennium expectations can, in turn, be traced back to Charles Grandison Finney, the most spectacular revivalist of the age. In 1835 Mr. Finney wrote, "If the Church would do her duty, the millennium may come to this country in three years." The millennium refers to a thousand-year reign of Christ that has been anticipated by many Christians since the beginning of the Christian era. Those who take this to mean a literal one-thousand-year reign on earth and build their hope on that understanding point to the text in Revelation 20:4–7. Trying to understand Revelation 20 has been the challenge for the Church in every generation. There have historically been several competing views this is to be interpreted.

Postmillennialism

First clearly articulated in America in the eighteenth century by its greatest theologian, Jonathan Edwards (1703–1758), postmillennialism and its understanding of Revelation 20 is one that embraces a hopeful and optimistic view of Jesus' thousand-year reign. Edwards and postmillennialists believed that through the influence of Christ, and the Christian message, the future would bring a time of peace, joy, and prosperity. It teaches that society could be redeemed by faith, hope, and charity. This viewpoint inspired such hymns as "The Battle Hymn of the Republic," which became popular by expressing an optimistic message:

> Mine eyes have seen the glory of the coming of the Lord / He is trampling out the vintage where the grapes of wrath are stored / He hath loosed the fateful lightning of his terrible swift sword / His truth is marching on.

Postmillennialists are not settled on when the return of Christ is set to happen, with some seeing the millennium reign of Christ currently happening.

Premillennialism

Others believed that the millennium was a definite period of time which would be inaugurated by the return of Christ to earth. The earth was not going to get better and better until the Lord came. The beginning of the millennial, not the end, was associated with the Second Advent.

An Unknown Hour

What everyone seemed to agree upon was that Jesus Christ was coming a second time for all who believed, according to promise (Heb. 9:28). What many wanted to know was, "When would the Second Advent take place? Jesus had taught in Matthew 24:36 "But of that day and hour knoweth no man, no, not the angels of heaven, but my Father only." Tragically, some individuals did not let the matter rest there, but insisted that the day, and the hour, and the year of the Lord's Second Advent can be known. One such person was William Miller.

Preparation of a Discredited "Prophet"

William Miller was born on February 15, 1782, in Pittsfield, Massachusetts. When he was four years old, William's family moved to rural Low Hampton, New York. Young Miller was educated at home by his mother until the age of nine, when he attended the newly established East Poultney District School. William is not known to have undertaken any type of formal study after the age of eighteen, though he continued to read widely and voraciously. In 1803, at the age of 21, Miller married Lucy Smith, and moved to her nearby hometown of Poultney, Vermont, where he took up farming. Miller enjoyed financial success as a farmer, and success in local politics as well.

Delighting in Deism

But not all was well with his spiritual life. Shortly after his move to Vermont, William Miller rejected his Baptist heritage, and became a deist. A desist is one who believes a Supreme Being created the universe, but has left it to operate according to fixed natural laws. In deism, reason can replace faith and organized religion. Many deists rejected the notion that God intervenes in human affairs through miracles and revelations, which also means the Bible was not to be fully trusted. In his biography, Mr. Miller explained why he forsook the God of his mother and his father at a critical time of his life. "I became acquainted with the principal men in that village [of Poultney, Vermont], who were professedly deists; but they were good citizens, and of a moral and serious deportment. They put into my hands the works of Voltaire, [David] Hume, Thomas Paine, Ethan Allen, and other such writers."

Mr. Miller was doomed to wander in spiritual darkness for several years. He joined the Masons and went on to seek happiness in social prominence, and in patriotism.

Fighting in the War of 1812

As a patriot, when war came in 1812 between the United States and England, William Miller raised a company of local militia and was awarded the rank of lieutenant. On February 1, 1814 he was promoted to captain. Captain Miller saw his first action on September 11, 1814, at the Battle of Plattsburgh (called the Battle of Champlain) in New York, where vastly outnumbered American forces overcame the British redcoats. In the providence of God, this particular battle became the occasion for William Miller to change his mind about spiritual matters.

A Change of Mind

"The fort I was in was exposed to every shot. Bombs, rockets, and shrapnel shells fell as thick as hailstones," he said. One of these many shots had exploded two feet from him, wounding three of his men, and killing another, but Miller survived without a scratch. William Miller came to view the outcome of this battle as miraculous, and therefore inconsistent with his deistic view of a distant God, far removed from human affairs. He later wrote, "It seemed to me that the Supreme Being must have watched over the interests of this country in an especial manner, and delivered us from the hands of our enemies... So surprising a result, against such odds, did seem to me like the work of a mightier power than man."

Finding Faith While Farming

After the war, and following his discharge from the army, on June 18, 1815, William Miller returned to Poultney, Vermont, and took up farming. But the thoughts of Mr. Miller were not wholly on farming. William Miller had become deeply concerned with the question of death, and an afterlife. This reflection upon his own mortality followed the sudden deaths of his father and sister, and his experiences as a soldier in the war. Initially, William Miller came to the conclusion there were only two options possible following death: annihilation, or, accountability before God; neither of which he was comfortable with. What was he to do? At first Mr. Miller attempted to combine both, publicly espousing deism, while simultaneously attending the local Baptist Church. His attendance turned to participation when he was asked to read a sermon when the local minister was absent. One Sunday, when he was reading a sermon about Christ, he became choked with emotion. Miller records the experience:

> Suddenly the character of a Savior was vividly impressed upon my mind. It seemed that there might be a Being so good and compassionate as to Himself atone for our transgressions, and thereby save us from suffering the

penalty of sin. I immediately felt how lovely such a Being must be; and imagined that I could cast myself into the arms of, and trust in the mercy of, such a One.

Regenerated by the grace of God, illuminated by the Holy Spirit, William Miller was converted to Christ.

Following his conversion, Miller was immediately challenged by his deist friends to justify his new-found faith. He did so by examining the Bible closely, declaring to one friend, "If you give me time, I will harmonize all apparent contradictions to my own satisfaction, or I will be a deist still." Miller began with Genesis 1:1, studying each verse of the text, and not moving on until he felt the meaning was clear. In this way he became convinced of two great concepts.

First, William Miller became convinced that the theological construct known as post-millennialism was inaccurate. Second, William Miller became convinced that the exact time of Christ's Second Coming was revealed in Bible prophecy.

Dismissing postmillennialism was easy to do because it was too optimistic. The concept of society becoming better and better, bringing forth a golden age of human history, was undermined by war, disease, and political unrest.

In dismissing postmillennialism, the heart of Mr. Miller became unguarded. There was danger for him at this critical point, as there is danger for all people who become disappointed. If the heart is not guarded, it is easy to become, not only disillusioned with the Church, but disgusted with the Church to the point that, the most glorious institution on earth is held in fundamental contempt. With the rejection of post millennialism because of its tremendous optimism about the future, Mr. Miller was suddenly open to another theological construct that finds the Church, not just corrupt, but an apostate organization, doomed for failure. The idea that the Church is an apostate organization doomed for failure was certainly not the thinking of Christ who "loved the Church, and gave himself for it; 26 That he might sanctify and cleanse it with the washing of water by the word, 27 That he might present it to himself a glorious Church, not having spot, or wrinkle, or any such thing; but that it should be holy and without blemish" (Eph. 5:25–27).

I would exhort God's people never to say that Christ's Church is going to fail, and do not believe those who say it will. Whatever faults the Church of the Living Lord might have, and they are significant, it is still a "glorious Church" in the heart of God the Father, God the Son, and God the Holy Spirit. The promise is given that the gates of hell shall *not* prevail against it. If a local assembly needs correction and cleansing, the Lord knows how to instruct or chastise His own, reflected in Paul's epistles to the local assemblies, and the Lord's messages to the seven Churches of the Revelation.

Disrespect and Defiance

There was something else Mr. Miller was open to, and that was a willingness to defy the teaching of Christ. A fundamental disrespect for the Church, will naturally lead to a fundamental disrespect for the Leader of the Church, Jesus Christ. Though Jesus Christ forbids the setting of dates, William Miller began to do just that.

The reason Mr. Miller was willing to defy the Lord Jesus Christ, was because of an old familiar sin, the sin of pride. One day in his spiritual journey, William Miller came to believe he had found a key to unlocking the great mystery of the timing of Christ's second coming—despite what Jesus has taught on this matter. While studying the book of Daniel, Mr. Miller came upon the words of the prophet in chapter 8 and verse 14. His mind was arrested by the words: "And he [the angel of the Lord] said unto me, Unto two thousand and three hundred days; then shall the sanctuary be cleansed."

Starting Down the Slippery Road

It is at this critical point that William Miller started down the slippery slope to biblical error, if not heterodoxy, for a thought came to him that the cleansing of the sanctuary referred to the earth's purification by fire at Christ's Second Coming. Such a simple thought it was, but it was to have far reaching negative consequences.

There is nothing in the biblical text to suggest that Daniel was shown a prophecy about Christ's Second Coming. Conservative biblical scholarship contends that the context has nothing to do with the purification of the earth, but it has everything to do with the defilement of the temple under Antiochus Epiphanes (lit.

"the Illustrious") and the cleansing of the Holy Temple. The events anticipated by Daniel were actually historical events by the time William Miller was alive. Mr. Miller should have studied Daniel 8 in light of the historical record. He should have examined the collected works of Josephus, read in the Apocrypha 1 Maccabees 4:52, and consulted Matthew Henry's *Commentary*, or even the words of John Calvin. There is a lesson to learn. When a person rejects the testimony of history, dismisses a natural reading of the Bible, and ignores the wisdom of Godly commentators, they set themselves up for foolishness, and a fall.

Two Mistakes in Interpreting the Bible

If the first mistake of William Miller was to ignore the grammatical and historical setting of the biblical text and assume that the passage referred to the Second Coming of Christ, his second mistake was to arbitrarily insist that the "2,300 days" were not literal, 24-hour days, but were instead 2,300 *years*. William Miller arbitrarily assumed that each *day* really stood for a *year*.

How did William Miller come up with the idea of a day for a year principle? Part of the answer lies in four other passages of Scripture, where a day for a year principle is declared.

The first passage is Numbers 14:34. "After the number of the days in which ye searched the land, even forty days, each day for a year, shall ye bear your iniquities, even forty years, and ye shall know my breach of promise."

Many centuries later, speaking to the prophet Ezekiel, the Lord told him the following. "[Ezekiel,] I have laid upon thee the years of their iniquity, according to the number of the days, three hundred and ninety days: so shalt thou bear the iniquity of the house of Israel" (Ezek. 4:5).

In Ezekiel 4:6, the Lord said, "And when thou hast accomplished them, lie again on thy right side, and thou shalt bear the iniquity of the house of Judah forty days: I have appointed thee each day for a year."

Finally, there is 2 Peter 3:8. "But, beloved, be not ignorant of this one thing, that one day is with the Lord as a thousand years, and a thousand years as one day."

An Important Difference

Sometimes, the day for a year principle is valid. But notice something very important. The difference between the passages in Numbers, Ezekiel and 2 Peter, and the passage in Daniel, is this. When God wanted to establish the day for a year principle, He said so. In Daniel 8:14 God does not indicate that a day equals a year, and so the commentator of Scripture must be careful not to read into the text what is not warranted. The text does speak of a time period of 2,300 days. Period. One day follows the next. The day for a year motif does not fit in this passage.

With two pre-suppositional thoughts firmly fixed in his mind, William Miller returned to Daniel 8:14, and decided that the 2,300 days of years period started in 457 BC with the decree to rebuild Jerusalem by Artaxerxes I of Persia. Simple calculation brought Mr. Miller to the conclusion that 2,300 years later, from

457 BC, would bring everyone to the year 1843. Oh, to think, in the year 1818, that by 1843, Jesus Christ was coming again!

The Key

William Miller records what he thought about the "key" that had been given to him in 1818, leading to what he was convinced, was a great discovery, regarding the time of the Second Advent. I doubt if the recorded thought William Miller left behind, actually conveyed the excitement in his heart. "I was thus brought . . . to the solemn conclusion, that in about twenty-five years from that time 1818, all the affairs of our present state would be wound up."

In 1818, William Miller was convinced of his calculations that Jesus was coming again in 1843. Nevertheless, he continued to study privately until 1823, to ensure the "correctness" of his interpretation.

Error has a tendency to reinforce itself, especially, if that error has its origin in the world, the flesh, or the devil.

In September 1822, William Miller formally stated his conclusions in a twenty-point document, including article 15: "I believe that the Second Coming of Jesus Christ is near, even at the door, even within twenty-one years—on or before 1843."

During these years of study, William Miller did not lecture in public about his Second Advent discovery, until the first Sunday in August, 1831, in the town of Dresden, New York. Needless to say, his sensational thoughts created a stir within the body of Christ.

The public response was one of intense excitement. Soon, the pressure was on to be more precise as to the exact time of the Lord's return. In response to public pressures, Mr. Miller began to narrow the time-period of the Second Advent to sometime in the Jewish year, beginning in the Gregorian year 1843. Said Mr. Miller, "My principles in brief, are, that Jesus Christ will come again to this earth, cleanse, purify, and take possession of the same, with all the saints, sometime between March 21, 1843, and March 21, 1844." Miller gave himself a one-year period of flexibility. If the first date did not work out, there was time to set new target dates. This is exactly what happened.

Miscalculation

The first day of expectation, March 21, 1843, passed without incident. As anticipated, after further discussion and study, a new date was set: April 18, 1843. This new date was based on the conservative Karaite Jewish calendar which is based on a lunar-solar month. Like the previous date, April 18, 1843, also passed without Christ's return. Soon thereafter, William Miller responded publicly, writing, "I confess my error, and acknowledge my disappointment; yet I still believe that the day of the Lord is near, even at the door." He would set no more dates. But others would.

In August, 1844, at a camp-meeting in Exeter, New Hampshire, Samuel S. Snow presented a message that became known as the "Seventh-Month" message, or the "True Midnight Cry." In a discussion based on scriptural typology, Samuel Snow presented his contorted conclusion, which was also based on the

2,300 day-year principle of the prophecy in Daniel 8:14 that Christ would return on, "the tenth day of the seventh month of the present year, 1844."

Another date was determined for the Lord's Second Coming: October 22, 1844. All the Millerites had to do was embrace the fact they were in the "Tarrying Time". This new terminology of hope was based on the words in Habakkuk 2:3. "For the vision is yet for an appointed time, but at the end it shall speak, and not lie: though it tarry, wait for it; because it will surely come, it will not tarry".

The Great Disappointment

When the sun rose on the morning of October 23, 1844, like any other day, confirming the Lord's coming had not taken place, there was incredible sadness. The previous day, the day of great expectation for the return of Jesus, October 22, 1844 suddenly became the Millerites' "Day of Great Disappointment."

Hiram Edson recorded that "Our fondest hopes and expectations were blasted, and such a spirit of weeping came over us as I never experienced before . . . We wept, and wept, till the day dawn." Following the Great Disappointment, most Millerites simply gave up their beliefs. Some did not, leading to new sensational viewpoints. Explanations proliferated to spin the failed prophesies. William Miller initially thought that Christ's Second Coming was still going to take place. He wrote that "the year of expectation was according to prophecy; but . . . that there might be an error in Bible chronology, which was of human origin, that could throw the date off somewhat and account for the discrepancy."

William Miller never gave up his belief in the Second Coming of Christ in his lifetime. He died on December 20, 1849 (age 67), still convinced that the Second Coming was imminent, not impending, but imminent. That word, imminent, is still found in the consciousness of the Christian community, and continues to inspire unreasonable expectations, while instilling fear and sensationalism into the hearts of countless millions. Mr. Miller is buried near his home in Low Hampton, New York, and his home is a registered National Historic Landmark and preserved as a museum. May the Lord help us to learn some practical and important lessons from the life of William Miller.

Practical Lessons from the Life of William Miller

First, let the Church remember that Error is bold, and it is militant. What began as a novel idea, gained ascendency through dogmatism, and persistency, to gain credibility, and, ultimately, a widespread acceptance. What the erroneous theory of evolution has done in secular society, the erroneous theories of eschatology have done in the Church. The result has been doctrinal havoc, confusion, division, and much falsehood.

Second, the setting of dates is prohibited in principle, and practice, by the word of God, and is unnecessary. In principle, trying to discern the future is associated with divination, which is condemned. "There shall not be found among you any one that maketh his son or his daughter to pass through the fire, or that useth divination, or an observer of times, or an enchanter, or a witch" (Deut. 18:10).

The Law of Moses prohibited every form of divination, because a prying into the future clouds the mind with superstition, and fanciful interpretations of Scripture, and it inclines the heart towards idolatry, specifically the idolatry of an inordinate love of a man and his ideas.

For a while, Mr. Miller was idolized, and anyone who spoke against him and his prophetic interpretation of the Scripture was angrily condemned. Go to Utah, and you will sense an inordinate worship and idolization of Joseph Smith. Go to Boston, to the Mother Church of Christian Science, and you will find idolization of Mary Glover Patterson Eddy. Go to the Islamic community, and you will find an inordinate love for the prophet Mohammed.

To tell the whole truth about Mohammed as a man, is to disrespect him, in the minds of many devout Muslims, and to risk having your throat slashed, and your head cut off, literally.

In the ancient world people used animal entrails, and omens, to foretell the future. Joseph Smith used "peepstones," and a hat. He bowed his head, and saw the future. You can read what he saw in the *Book of Mormon*, the *Pearl of Great Price*, and *Doctrine and Covenants*.

Today, individuals use the television, the internet, modern technology, and four blood moons to foretell the future. This practice is dangerous, and it is forbidden.

Despite God's prohibition on the setting of dates and the seeking of signs, individuals in the Church, in every century, have engaged in this practice.

Christian people, who know better, still set dates for the return of Christ, or come perilously close to doing so to the extent it is hard to see how they are not guilty of violating the known will of God.

In 1979, in a Baptist Church in Dalton, Tennessee, I sat in the audience, and heard the former president of Dallas Theological Seminary, declare he fully intended to be alive for the Rapture of the Church, which he called Phase I of the Second Coming of Christ. Dr. Walvoord (b. May 1, 1910) died on December 20, 2002, terribly mistaken in a key doctrinal belief.

Then there is the prophetic writer Hal Lindsey (b. Nov. 23, 1929) who wrote a bestselling work, published in May 1970, *The Late Great Planet Earth*, and another one, *The 1980s: Countdown to Armageddon*. From a divine perspective, it is possible Hal Lindsey is in trouble, for he has spoken things in the name of the Lord which have not come to pass. That is a serious matter with God who is jealous for His name.

A third practical lesson, is that the Church must be careful what we read, and embrace, and teach others, for ideas have consequences. Every Christian must bring every thought into captivity for Christ. "Casting down imaginations, and every high thing that exalteth itself against the knowledge of God, and bringing into captivity every thought to the obedience of Christ" (2 Cor. 10:5). Had Mr. William Miller forgone his "eureka" moment, had he arrested his presuppositional thinking, had he studied what the Church has believed down through the centuries, the course of his life would have been far different. He would not have departed from the faith once delivered to the saints.

A fourth lesson to be reminded of, is that we as Christians must be careful of becoming so emotionally attached to a System of belief, that there is no room to be taught by the Holy Spirit, and thus to be led into the simple truth of God's Word. We must not dismiss the voice of the Church down through the centuries.

In the matter of eschatology, the Church has consistently taught two critical points. First, Jesus Christ is coming again in the same manner in which He went away. Literally, slowly, bodily, and visibly. "Which also said, Ye men of Galilee, why stand ye gazing up into heaven? This same Jesus, which is taken up from you into heaven, shall so come in like manner as ye have seen him go into heaven" (Acts 1:11). Second, Jesus Christ is coming again the second time for all who believe. "So Christ was once offered to bear the sins of many; and unto them that look for him shall he appear the second time without sin unto salvation" (Heb. 9:28).

A fifth lesson to remember, is that the good that men do is said to live after them, and so is the harm they do. Estimates of the number of followers of William Miller vary between 50,000, and 500,000. That is a lot of people to mislead, and give false hope to. What is worse, is that the spiritual legacy of Mr. Miller includes the Advent Christian Church with 61,000 members, the Seventh-day Adventist Church with over 8 million members, and the Jehovah Witnesses numbering 20 million adherents. These denominations have a direct connection with the Millerites, and the Great Disappointment of 1844. Beware, so that when your ministry is over, you have done no harm.

On the Positive Side

Though William Miller was wrong in his prophetic understanding of Scripture, he was strong in his love for Christ, and belief, that the Bible is the Word of God. It is possible for good men to have bad theology, and so we must remember to be gracious as we return to the Scriptures for all faith and practice. Despite the egregious doctrinal errors William Miller promoted, there was much good that came from his ministry.

Many souls were converted to Christ. Church attendance increased. Personal Bible study was emphasized. The morals of many communities improved. Multitudes began to ask themselves if they were ready to meet Christ. Local revival often followed the ministry of William Miller.

Finally, whatever divergent eschatological events and activities individuals believe might still happen, the discussion in prophetic matters should be covered by Christian charity. "But foolish and unlearned questions avoid, knowing that they do gender strifes." (2 Tim. 2:23)

> In essentials, unity;
>   in non-essentials, liberty;
> in all things, charity.
> —Rupertus Meldenius
> German Theologian, c. 1627

Ultimately, this is what I hope the Church will learn from the life of William Miller: Love Christ. Study the Scriptures. Study Church history. Be humble. Be teachable. Be careful. Be loving.

Had Mr. Miller consulted John Calvin's *Commentary* on Daniel 8:26, his error would have been arrested. "The expression, to evening and morning, is not doubtful, since Christ, clearly means two thousand three hundred days; for what else can the phrase, morning and evening, signify? It cannot be used of either years or months. Evidently, we ought to understand natural days here, consisting of twenty-four hours each. Those who receive it of years and months are wretchedly mistaken, and even ridiculous in their calculations."

Chapter 2

Are We in the Last Days?

"As I read the news, I can't help but wonder if we are in the last hours before our Lord Jesus Christ returns to rescue His Church, and God pours out His wrath on the world for the rejection of His Son," said Rev. Franklin Graham in a post on the Billy Graham Evangelistic Association (BGEA) website (September 4, 2014, CBS News). Mr. Graham went on to say, "I don't know if we have hours, days, months, or years—but as Christians, God calls us to take the truth of the Gospel to the ends of the earth."

For more than fifty years, I have warned the Church against reading the newspapers and looking at current events in order to derive one's eschatology. There are several reasons why it is unwise to wonder, believe, predict, or teach prophetically that the world is in "the last hours before our Lord Jesus Christ returns."

First, idle wonderings leading to prophetic speculation is a manifestation of wickedness and spiritual adultery. Jesus said that "A wicked and adulterous generation seeketh after a sign; and there shall no sign be given unto it, but the sign of the prophet

Jonas. And he left them, and departed" (Matt. 16:4). This generation, and Americans in particular, must be among the most wicked, and most adulterous generation that has ever lived, for seeking for the signs of the time for the Lord's second coming is a national passion. Countless prophetic pundits flood the airwaves, television, and social media with incessant doomsday predictions—and they are all consistently wrong.

Second, prophetic speculation shows a naivete regarding human history. Former president Barak Obama was not wrong when he said that the world has always been messy. While the former President is right in that observation, it is also true, that in the midst of "messiness" some great civilizations have perished because the leaders partied rather than attended to urgent national concerns. The biblical story of the fall of the great city of Babylon, recorded in Daniel 5, offers one example of a national calamity occurring while the leaders of government were busy with self-centered and self-serving activities—equivalent to the modern practice of playing golf, or raising money, and banqueting, while the world falls apart around them.

Third, prophetic speculation instills unnecessary fear into the hearts of people. God has not given His people a spirit of fear, but power, love, and a sound mind. "For God hath not given us the spirit of fear; but of power, and of love, and of a sound mind" (2 Tim. 1:7). One of the signs of a false prophet, was that he instilled fear in the hearts of people by predicting events that did not come to pass, but that raised alarm. "When a prophet speaketh in the name of the Lord, if the thing follows not, nor come to pass, that is the thing which the Lord hath not spoken, but the prophet hath spoken it presumptuously: thou shalt not be afraid of him" (Deut. 18:22).

Fourth, most prophetic wondering, and speculation, is based on unbiblical expectations and theories. The Bible teaches that all of humanity has been living in the "last days" since the days of the apostles. "Little children, it is the last time: and as ye have heard that antichrist shall come, even now are there many antichrists; whereby we know that it is the last time" (1 John 2:18).

The idea of Christ coming to rescue his Church prior to a final pouring out of His wrath on the world, is code language for a theological construct known as Dispensationalism. Those who embrace Dispensational teaching believe that the Church will be Raptured prior to a period of great suffering on earth. Dispensationalism is a complex teaching that has developed in detail since the 1830s, but it is not a historical teaching of the Church, nor are the main propositions of Dispensationalism rooted in sound biblical theology. The "System" keeps changing. Today there is something known as "Progressive Dispensationalism." Truth does not change. The hope of the Rapture does nothing to prepare the Church for the experience of tribulation, which Jesus, and the apostles, warned about.

Jesus said that His followers would know tribulation. "These things I have spoken unto you, that in me ye might have peace. In the world ye shall have tribulation: but be of good cheer; I have overcome the world" (John 16:33). The apostle Paul said that he confirmed the Church by reminding them of tribulation. "Confirming the souls of the disciples, and exhorting them to continue in the faith, and that we must through much tribulation enter into the kingdom of God" (Acts 14:22).

No one has a right to put fear into the hearts of God's people with idle speculation about the time of the return of Jesus Christ. No one has a right to place the Lord's return within a definite framework, as foolish people have consistently done throughout the ages. No one, especially a prominent religious leader, has a right to publicly offer false hope of escaping tribulation to Christians, even in coded language. Whatever private concerns a person might have about Armageddon, whatever "hoof beats" of the four riders of the Apocalypse a person might believe they are hearing, let that person take their fears and apprehensions to the Lord in prayer, and then open the Scriptures to receive comfort.

> When thou pass through the waters, I will be with thee; and through the rivers, they shall not overflow thee: when thou walkest through the fire, thou shalt not be burned; neither shall the flame kindle upon thee (Isa. 43:2).

> Blessed be God, even the Father of our Lord Jesus Christ, the Father of mercies, and the God of all comfort; Who comforteth us in all our tribulation, that we may be able to comfort them which are in any trouble, by the comfort wherewith we ourselves are comforted of God. 5 For as the sufferings of Christ abound in us, so our consolation also aboundeth by Christ (2 Cor. 1:3–5).

The world has known worldwide calamities before. There is the story of World War I. There is the story of World War II to remember. The conflict between Russia and the Ukraine, the rise of militant Islam, the civil wars in Syria, Iran, Libya, and Egypt should easily remind Christians to remember the words of our Lord. "And ye shall hear of wars and rumors of wars: see that ye be not troubled: for all these things must come to pass, but the end is not yet. For nation shall rise against nation, and kingdom against kingdom: and there shall be famines, and pestilences, and earthquakes, in divers places. All these are the beginning of sorrows" (Matt. 24:6–8).

No matter what human history proves to be, Jesus is still the Lord of history, and all shall be well.

> When peace, like a river, attendeth my way,
> When sorrows like sea billows roll;
> Whatever my lot, Thou hast taught me to say,
> It is well, it is well with my soul.
> It is well, with my soul,
> It is well, it is well, with my soul.
> —Horatio Spafford

Chapter 3

Why Do So Many People Believe in the Rapture?

"For the Lord himself shall descend from heaven with a shout, with the voice of the archangel, and with the trump of God: and the dead in Christ shall rise first: Then we which are alive and remain shall be caught up together with them in the clouds, to meet the Lord in the air: and so shall we ever be with the Lord. Wherefore comfort one another with these words" (1 Thess. 4:16–18).

"There is neither Jew nor Greek, there is neither bond nor free, there is neither male nor female: for ye are all one in Christ Jesus" (Gal. 3:28).

Forty years prior to the fall of Jerusalem in A.D. 70, the Lord Jesus Christ warned that in the midst of the great tribulation period which would come upon the generation to which He spoke (Matt. 24:32; Mark 13:30) false Christs and false prophets would arise to speak of His secret, silent return. The purpose of this teaching would be in order to seduce, if it were possible, even the elect (Mark 13:22). "But take ye heed: behold, I have foretold you all things."

As Jesus predicted, there were false Messiahs who appeared, such as John of Gischala (A.D. 66–70). The historical record states, "Now as Josephus was thus engaged in the administration of the affairs of Galilee, there arose a treacherous person, a man of Gischala, the son of Levi, whose name was John." John was a man full of ambitions. He saw that he could make a name for himself by going to Jerusalem to rally the people to resist the Romans. "On John's arrival, the whole populace of Jerusalem turned out, crying for news of events outside." Seizing the moment, John "went round urging them [the citizens of Jerusalem] one and all to war by false hopes, making out that Roman power was feeble, exaggerating Jewish strength, and ridiculing the ignorance of those who were worried." Said John, "Not even if they grew wings could the Romans ever get over the walls of Jerusalem, after being so severely mauled in their attacks on Galilean villages and wearing out their engines against flimsy walls" (Josephus, Book IV, *The Jewish War*).

Amazingly enough, many people believed the words of John. The people in fear hoped against hope—and the power and influence of John, son of Levi, escalated. He was the Man of the Hour. He was to be the Savior of the Jewish people. Or, so many thought. In the end John was overthrown, and his power was broken, but not before he had misled many into thinking he was the Messiah.

Like the Jews of old, who followed anyone who pretended to know something about the return of Christ, or hope for the future in the midst of social uncertainty, many today are falling into great error, we believe, by following after those who pretend to know that Christ is here, or is coming there, in 1975, 1981, 1988, October 21, 2011, etc. With great authority God's people are being told that this is the Terminal Generation, and that the coming of Christ is imminent.

According to many modern Dispensational teachings, the next event on the prophetic calendar is the Rapture of the Church, which will lead to the revelation of the Antichrist. The Antichrist, it is alleged, will give a plausible explanation for the disappearance of millions of Christians.

Being a charismatic leader with a strong personality, the Antichrist will win the confidence of the world, especially after war breaks out in the Middle East, and he is able to make peace for Israel.

Unfortunately, as the storyline goes, the Antichrist cannot be trusted, for his will to power is without boundaries. He marks on the forehead of people his number, which is 666. No one can buy or sell except they agree to worship this Beast.

The political treaty the Antichrist has made with Israel will be broken after only three-and-a-half years. This breaking of the treaty will then lead the nations of the world to converge upon Israel for the great Battle of Armageddon. It will be a violent and bloody conflict. Blood will flow freely to the height of a horse's bridle.

The evidence for all this teaching, and more, is said to be rooted in Scripture. However, if these things are taught in Scripture, they are not taught clearly. In other words, the average reader of the Bible cannot just go to the Word of God, open it up, and see these prophecies clearly set forth. Nevertheless, trusting those who believe they have the gift of prophetic insight, millions are embracing something they cannot comprehend for themselves. Unlike the Bereans, who searched the Scriptures to see whether or not the things Paul taught were rooted in the Word, God's people accept what they cannot conceive. Acts 17:11-12, "Now the Bereans were of more noble character than the Thessalonians, for they received the message with great eagerness and examined the Scriptures every day to see if what Paul said was true."

My first question is this: Why do so many people believe in the Rapture of the Church, the rise of Antichrist, a peace treaty to be made with Israel, the rebuilding of the Jewish Temple, the revival of the ancient Roman Empire, and the battle of Armageddon, including China, and Russia when none of these concepts are clearly and simply set forth in plain language in the Bible? Furthermore, Why are Christians not willing to be more like the Bereans, and less like the Jews of old, who followed the charismatic false Messiah and teacher, John of Gadara?

Apart from not being clearly seen in the Scriptures, the main points of Dispensational teachings are of dubious origin. A great search has been launched to discover when the Church first began to hear that the second coming of Christ was not really one great event for all that believe (Heb. 9:28), but was to take place in two stages, separated by an interval of time.

President John F. Kennedy once remarked that failure is an orphan while success has many claimants. Since Dispensational teaching has been successful in capturing the imaginations of men, and changing historic Christian doctrine, it has many parents. For example, John Nelson Darby claimed he received his revelation of the Rapture in 1827 when he realized the distinction between Israel and the Church. Critics of John Darby accused him of taking his prophetic ideas from Edward Irving, a Presbyterian pastor in London.

Others, however, suggest that a fifteen-year-old girl named Margaret MacDonald, of Port Glasgow, Scotland, should be credited to have originated the concept of the Rapture in 1830, which was picked up by the Brethren Movement and made their own.

Some Church historians credit Emmanuel Lacunza, a Jesuit Catholic priest, of first teaching a two-stage coming of Christ, separated by a period of time in 1812 in his book, *The Coming of Messiah in Glory and Majesty*. Another book published in England in 1788 (but written c. 1742–44), purports to have taught the pre-tribulation Rapture before Lacunza.

Whoever is to be credited with the seed thought that the coming of Christ is to be in two stages, separated by a period of time, that person has done the cause of Christ much harm, and has brought great confusion into the Church. In light of this, a second question arises. "Why do so many people believe in the Rapture of the Church, when the language used to describe that, and the Second Coming, is incredulous and non-sensible?" At no other time do people talk about going somewhere in two stages, separated by a period of time, and calling everything one event.

Years ago, I drove from Pennsylvania to Fort Worth, Texas to see my son, who was serving on a naval base in that city. Image the reaction to this conversation at the end of the first visit. "Son, I am going to come back a second time. However, my coming will be in two stages—separated by several years. In the first phase of my return, I will draw near the city in secret, with a great shout, and then disappear, but in the second phase you will plainly see me. But remember, I am only going to come a second time."

If my son had said he understood what I was saying I would have been worried about him. If he did not comprehend what I had said I would be more impressed, for it means he realizes that my words were illogical and non-sensible.

Apart from the inability to see the prophetic teachings of Dispensationalism clearly in the Scriptures like the Bereans, and apart from the fact the language used to describe The System of belief is non-sensible, there is another concern. The Rapture theory makes God the Father out to be less than truthful. If that is shocking, it is meant to be, but it is also a fact.

Relatively few people understand where the belief in a seven-year tribulation period comes from, so let me try to tell you. The story begins in Daniel 9:24–27. Daniel was but a young boy when he was taken into captivity together with three other Hebrew youths of nobility, Hananiah, Mishael, and Azariah, at the first deportation of the people of Judah, in the fourth year of Jehoiakim (604 B.C.).

Daniel and his companions were obliged to enter the service of the royal court of Babylon, on which occasion he received the Chaldean name Belteshazzar, according to the Eastern custom of taking a new name when a change takes place in one's condition of life, and more especially if his personal liberty is thereby affected (2 Kgs. 23:34; 24:17).

Daniel, like Joseph, gained the favor of his guardian, and was allowed by him to carry out his wise intention of abstaining from unclean food, and idolatrous ceremonies (Dan. 1:8–16). His prudent conduct, and absolute refusal to comply with heathen customs, were crowned with the divine blessing, and had important results.

After three years of training, Daniel was presented to the king, and shortly afterward he had an opportunity to exercise his peculiar gift (2 Kgs. 1:17) of interpreting dreams, not only recalling the forgotten vision of the king, but also revealing its meaning (2 Kgs. 2:14–45).

As a reward Daniel was made "ruler over the whole province of Babylon," and "chief prefect over all the wise men of Babylon" (Dan. 2:48). Later he interpreted another of Nebuchadnezzar's dreams to the effect that he was to lose for a time his throne but was to be restored to it after his humiliation had been completed (chap. 4). Under the unworthy successors of Nebuchadnezzar, Daniel appears to have occupied an inferior position (Dan. 8:27); no longer was he the "chief of the magicians" (Dan. 4:8–9). He was sent to live a quiet and obscure life in Susa (Dan. 8:2).

But all that was to change. In the first year of King Belshazzar (Dan. 7:1), about 555 B.C., Daniel was both alarmed and comforted by a remarkable vision (chap. 7), followed by another two years later (chap. 8), which disclosed to him the future course of events, and the ultimate fate of the most powerful empires of the world, in particular their relations to the kingdom of God, and its development to the great consummation.

Word of his prophetic gift began to circulate once more. And so it was that Daniel was brought in to interpret the handwriting on the wall that disturbed the feast of Belshazzar (Dan. 5:10-28), and, notwithstanding his bold denunciation of the king, the latter appointed him the "third ruler in the kingdom" (Dan. 5:29). After the fall of Babylon, Darius ascended the throne of the dominant kingdom in the Middle East, and made Daniel the first of the "three commissioners" of the new Persian Empire (Dan. 6:2). In deep humiliation, and prostration of spirit, Daniel then prayed to the Lord in the name of his people for forgiveness of their sins and for the divine mercy in their behalf; and the answering promises that he received far exceeded the tenor of his prayer, for the visions of the seer were extended to the end of Judaism (chap. 9) (see *The New Unger's Bible Dictionary*).

Of particular concern in these visions, is the fact that a timetable was given to Daniel. The prophet was told "that from the going forth of the commandment to restore and to build Jerusalem unto the Messiah the Prince shall be seven weeks, and threescore and two weeks: the street shall be built again, and the wall, even in troublous times" (Dan. 9:24-27). When the executive order was given to the Jews to return to their land and rebuild Jerusalem, from that moment forward it would be 490 years, and then the Messiah would come.

However, according to Dispensational teaching, God did not give the Jews 490 years on schedule as He promised. Rather, God gave the Jews 483 years of human history, and then "suspended" time until the Church could come into existence and be removed. With the removal of the Church the prophetic clock will start to "tick" again, and then, finally, God will keep His word to ancient Israel.

While this is an intriguing position to take, it does make God out to be less than truthful, for if accurate, it means that God promised the Jews 490 years, and only gave them 483 years. I suggest that rather than break the prophetic word—which Jesus said cannot be broken (John 10:35)—the Scriptures be accepted by faith that God kept His word, and after 490 years, in the fullness of time, Christ came (Eph. 1:10).

Now the third question is this: "Why do so many people believe in a system that makes God out to be less than truthful?" In a more charitable spirit, it can be said that people believe in the Rapture of the Church, and all of Dispensational teaching for a variety of reasons, some nobler than others.

Many Christians are convinced that Dispensational teaching reflects the doctrine of Scripture. Because so many passages of the Bible are alluded to in Dispensational teaching, it is easy to see why this would be the case.

Some Christians believe Dispensational teaching because they have been taught it all their lives, and do not want to test the spirits to see if they are of God or search the Scriptures as commanded. Other Christians are simply willing to trust their spiritual leaders not to mislead them.

There are additional reasons for a system of belief contrary to the historic Christian faith. It is possible for God's people to be misled by erroneous teaching. Galatians 1:6–7, "I marvel that ye are so soon removed from him that called you into the grace of Christ unto another gospel: Which is not another; but there be some that trouble you, and would pervert the gospel of Christ."

One form of judgment God renders, is to allow people to believe a lie. "And for this cause God shall send them strong delusion, that they should believe a lie" (2 Thess. 2:11).

Satan knows how to make doctrine appear to be an enlightened position. Therefore, it is no great thing if his ministers also be transformed as the ministers of righteousness; whose end shall be according to their works" (2 Cor. 11:15).

Without doubt one of the cleverest ways that Satan transforms truth, is by alluding to passages of Scripture that tend to support a position, but upon examination, has nothing to do with the topic of discussion. Let me give two examples.

First, it is a fundamental position of Dispensational teaching that God has two people, two plans, and two programs, one for the Jews, and another for the Church. "Israel is Israel, the Church is the Church, and never the two shall meet." At this point 1 Corinthians 10:32 is often quoted. "Give none offence, neither to the Jews, nor to the Gentiles, nor to the Church of God."

From this passage in 1 Corinthians 10:32, it is taught that God has a plan for (ethnic) Israel, distinct from the Church. This plan involves seven years of Tribulation, a peace treaty with the Antichrist, and all the rest. However, in context, eschatology is not in view in 1 Corinthians 10:32, nor is there some special plans for national Israel that is being discussed. What is taught, is that Christians should be careful not to offend anyone by causing the conscience to be violated.

Another example of taking a passage and making it mean something it does not, is Revelation 4:1. According to Dispensational thinking, John, representing the Church, is "Raptured" into heaven before the outpouring of divine wrath on earth. Therefore, it is argued, the Church must be removed during the Tribulation period. The problem with this teaching is that nothing of the sort is taught. Nowhere in Scripture is it ever said that John is a type of the Church. John was in the spirit on the Lord's Day. While his soul was allowed to see a vision, his body remained fixed firmly on the earth.

Furthermore, to suggest that the Church is not found in chapters 4–19 of the book of the Revelation, or during the alleged future tribulation period, borders on the incredulous. Christians are addressed in chapter 6:11 as fellow servants. Christians are called brethren in chapter 6:11. Those saints who die during the tribulation period are called "the dead who die in the Lord" in chapter 14:13. The Church is found in chapter 14, for we read of "the saints" in verse 12 and in Revelation 15:6 and again in 17:6. The Church is the called, chosen, and faithful of Revelation 17:14.

To teach that the Church is not found in Revelation 4–19 because it is "raptured" out of the way is something not found in Scripture.

The conclusion of the matter is this. In every local assembly there is a mixture of truth and error. However, when error begins to overshadow the historic Christian faith, and transform what has been articulated since the days of the apostles, such error must be challenged. God wants His people to study and to stay close to His Word. May the Lord give us grace to contend for the faith, while resisting being misled. Why, indeed, do so many people believe in the Rapture, when the victorious life, and the Second Coming of Christ are truths to be treasured?

Chapter 4

Inconsistency in the Rapture Theory

> "No one has ever accused Christians of being consistent."
> —Stanford E. Murrell

Those who know me well know that I enjoy ending teachable moments by summarizing a point with a "pithy statement," or a "mantra," for lack of a better word. While reading a recent issue of the "Sword of the Lord" magazine, I felt compelled to express such a mantra while reading the sermon with the title, "The Rapture" by Dr. B. R. Larkin.

To set the narrative, it must be understood that the "Sword of the Lord" is militant in its opposition to Calvinism. The Sword's current editor endorses and supports Sword Conferences dedicated to the denunciation of the doctrines of grace, despite the fact that the Christian publication often prints sermons by Charles Spurgeon who said the following:

> I have my own opinion that there is no such thing as preaching Christ and Him crucified, unless we preach

what nowadays is called Calvinism. It is a nickname to call it Calvinism; Calvinism is the gospel, and nothing else. I do not believe we can preach the gospel if we do not preach justification by faith without works; nor unless we preach the sovereignty of God in His dispensation of grace; nor unless we exalt the electing unchangeable eternal, immutable, conquering love of Jehovah; nor do I think we can preach the gospel unless we base it upon the special and particular redemption of His elect and chosen people which Christ wrought out upon the cross (Charles Spurgeon, *The New Park Street Pulpit*, Vol. 1, 1856).

One reason the Sword of the Lord's Editor and fellow contributors take a strong stand against Calvinism, is a mistaken belief that the doctrines of grace discourage sinners from coming to Christ. Another reason, is a misguided notion the doctrines of grace hinder soul winning efforts. A third reason, is a false belief that Calvinism teaches only a select few can be saved.

In this same issue, in a boldly lined large box to attract special attention, an antidote is given with the title "William Booth on Calvinism." Apparently, Mr. Booth was once given a book "which fully explained the doctrine." What was Mr. Booth's reaction to the book? The narrative continues. "I threw it at the wall opposite me and said I would sooner starve than to preach such a doctrine, one special feature of which was that only a select few could be saved."

Of course, by way of a brief defense, the doctrines of grace do not teach that "only a select few could be saved." The doctrines of grace clearly teach the arms of God are opened wide. Let every sinner listen to the divine gospel call: "Ho, every one that thirsteth, come ye to the waters, and he that hath no money; come ye, buy, and eat; yea, come, buy wine and milk without money and without price" (Isa. 55:1). Hear the Savior Himself cry out, "If any man thirst, let him come unto me, and drink. 38 He that believeth on me, as the scripture hath said, out of his belly shall flow rivers of living water" (John 7:37-38). The question is not who "could" be saved, but who will be saved, and on what basis? That is the point where a good biblically based discussion should begin. But I digress.

The larger point, I would like to note, is that while our Arminian Dispensational brethren viscerally denounce the biblical doctrine of election, they have no problem recognizing, and promoting an elect people in another area, in as far as they believe it benefits their theological bias regarding an alleged Rapture, that is ostensibly to take place seven years prior to the return of Christ to earth. I refer now to the sermon by Dr. B. R. Larkin who said, "Only a select few will be caught up in the clouds—only those who are 'in Christ.' Nobody knows the number of people who will be saved in that day. But Jesus didn't encourage us to believe that just everybody would go when He said, 'As the days of Noe were, so shall also the coming of the Son of man be' (Matt. 24:37).... No, the Rapture will be selective. It is strictly, and only for those who are 'in Christ'."

While denouncing there is an elect people in regard to salvation, our Christian brethren insist there is an elect people in regard to the Rapture. Only those who are "in Christ" will be in the

Rapture—which parallels what Calvinist teach, only those in Christ shall be saved.

Because they limit the Rapture to the elect, or those in Christ, should our Arminian Dispensational brethren be accused of not wanting to see souls saved? Are they not plainly teaching that only the elect, only the few, will be in the Rapture, thereby discouraging all other souls from going up? The concept of a special, select, elect people that is denounced in one area, is it not being affirmed in another?

I say again, no one ever accused Christians of being consistent. No wonder multitudes are confused, and feel "left behind."

Chapter 5

Will the Bride of Christ Be Raptured?

"So that we ourselves glory in you in the Churches of God for your patience and faith in all your persecutions and tribulations that ye endure: Which is a manifest token of the righteous judgment of God, that ye may be counted worthy of the kingdom of God, for which ye also suffer" (2 Thess. 1:4–5).

There is a wildly popular teaching called the Rapture, which declares that the Church, as the Bride of Christ, will not go through a seven-year tribulation period, which is soon to come. Anne Graham Lotz, daughter of evangelist Billy Graham, made headline news around the world when she articulated this point of view.

> ANNE GRAHAM LOTZ, THE DAUGHTER OF THE REV. BILLY GRAHAM, WARNS THE RAPTURE IS COMING AND WILL CAUSE "MASS CHAOS"

In a recent blog posted on her website titled "Is God's Judgment Coming?" Graham Lotz wrote God's "judgment is coming on America and on our world, and it's going to be ugly."

"I believe Jesus is soon to return to take all of His followers to Heaven with Him in what is referred to as the Rapture," she wrote. "While this will be deliverance for His people, can you imagine the impact on our nation, let alone the world, when suddenly every single authentic Christian disappears?" ("Newsmax", May 21, 2015).

Anne Graham Lotz is a good woman, with a good heart, but she has some very questionable, and unorthodox theology, in a variety of important areas, despite holding six honorary doctorates. Mrs. Lotz is one of many modern-day prophetic teachers giving false hope to Christians, especially in the Western world, by promising divine deliverance through disappearance, while Christians in the Middle East spill their blood in the sand for being faithful to their Lord and Saviour, Jesus Christ.

Anne Graham Lotz speaks of deliverance, by Rapture, for "His people," referring to Christians. But are not the suffering saints in the Middle East, "His people" too? Are they not Christians? Are they not the Bride of Christ? Indeed, they are.

Because Christians in the Middle East are part of the Church, let them hear the same gospel promise given to the suffering saints of the first century going through great tribulation. Let the word go forth. The Church of Christ shall emerge triumphant over the forces of evil. Dear suffering Christian, whoever you are, wherever you are, your testimony shall not be in vain. For Christ "must reign, till he hath put all enemies under his feet" (1 Cor. 15:25).

And, if the Lord asks you to be a witness even unto death, be faithful, for you shall yet live. John wrote, "And I saw thrones, and they sat upon them, and judgment was given unto them: and I saw the souls of them that were beheaded for the witness of Jesus, and for the word of God, and which had not worshipped the beast, neither his image, neither had received his mark upon their foreheads, or in their hands; and they lived and reigned with Christ a thousand years" (Rev. 20:4). Suffering Christian, you shall live, and reign with God.

People like Anne Graham Lotz, who embrace the Rapture of the Church, base their understanding on a false premise. The false premise is that Christians will escape the great tribulation. The word tribulation is found at least twenty-six times in the Authorized Version, and each time the Bible assures believers that tribulation shall be part of the Christian experience.

Jesus said, "In the world ye shall have tribulation" (John 16:33). Paul taught the Church that Christians, "through much tribulation enter into the kingdom of God" (Acts 14:22). Nevertheless, the hope lives that the Bride of Christ will not go through any part of the great tribulation. Jesus said just the opposite.

The suffering Christians in the Middle East are a testimony to the truthfulness of Jesus, and the teaching of the apostles. Christians will, and do, suffer through all the great tribulations that come to nations, and they prevail. From A.D. 70 to the year 2015, Christians prevail, and they always come out of the great tribulation with the banner of Christ's love and faithfulness flying high.

"Ah," says the Dispensationalist. But we are talking about *the* great tribulation," though the Bible never uses the definite article when talking about tribulation. But what greater tribulation is there than to be beheaded for Christ? And that is now happening to the Bride of Christ. So do not talk about Christians escaping *the* great tribulation, while the blood of martyrs is still dripping.

An appeal is often made by prophetic pundits to 1 Thessalonians 5:9. The apostle Paul wrote, "For God hath not appointed us to wrath, but to obtain salvation by our Lord Jesus Christ."

For the Dispensationalist, the wrath Paul speaks in 1 Thessalonians 5:9 is the wrath of THE great tribulation, referring to a future seven-year period of special judgment. But this is a modern understanding based upon presuppositional conditioning.

The wrath of which Paul speaks is not a temporal wrath of seven years, but the eternal wrath of God on the wicked, who do not repent of sin.

Armed with a false hope of not suffering, and a misunderstanding of 1 Thessalonians 5:9, prophetic teachers, such as Anne Graham Lotz, can convey to others their erroneous beliefs, and false hopes.

"I believe that in my lifetime, if I live out my natural lifetime, I believe I will live to see the return of Jesus in the rapture when he comes back to take us to be with Himself, which means preceding that there are going to be some signs, there are going to be some warnings," she said. Then, with a slight acknowledgement to those who are suffering even unto death, Anne Graham Lotz, like all modern prophetic teachers, covers herself by saying, "And like the Israelites in Egypt when God sent the 10 plagues on

Egypt and forced Pharaoh to let His children go," she said, the Israelites also suffered under some of the plagues.

"They still came under some of the judgment," said Anne Graham Lotz. "So before Jesus comes back, He may allow the Church to go through some judgment because it purifies us. It helps us get our priorities straight and increases our focus and also our compulsion, I think, to share the Gospel with the people around us."

"They still came under some of the judgment?" Wait a minute. The System teaches that "His People", the "Bride of Christ" do not come under the judgment. They do not come under the wrath! The Rapture, of which Anne Graham Lotz believes, insists that the Bride of Christ is to be removed. The Church is not appointed to "some of the judgment."

That is the problem with erroneous teaching. It is impossible for everyone trying to teach it to be consistent. The System affirms what it denies, and denies what it affirms.

Here then, is the truth of the matter. The present beheading of Christians by ISIS, the stoning of believers, the confiscation of their property, false imprisonment, the destruction of Church property, and the driving of Christians into exile, is the tribulation of which Jesus foretold. The Bride of Christ is not appointed to eternal wrath, for the wrath of God is reserved for the nonbeliever. But Christians, through much tribulation, and in every generation, must enter into the kingdom of God.

It is irresponsible to give false hope to non-suffering Christians in the West, when the evidence abounds that the Bride of Christ is at this present hour going through great tribulation.

Ironically, an appeal for belief in the Rapture, whereby Christians leave, and the wicked are left behind, is based on the biblical illustrations of circumstances similar to those in the days of Noah, and the days of Lot. But something has been lost in the analogy, because in the days of Noah the wicked were taken, and the righteous were "left behind." Likewise, in the days of Lot, the wicked were taken, and the righteous were "left behind." When Dispensationalism gets through with the Scriptures, the analogy is turned upside down. The righteous are taken, and the wicked are "left behind."

There is something else. Neither Noah, nor Lot, and those associated with the righteous were removed from earth. They went through the difficult days, and were preserved. During these dark days, when the Bride of Christ is caught up in the wrath of God being poured out upon the Islamic nations in the Middle East, as the LORD of Hosts moves Arab to kill Arab, to reflect the bloodlust of their god Allah, the Christians will emerge triumphant. The prophet Mohammed is dead. Osama Bin Laden is dead. ISIS shall also be destroyed. All who oppose Christ and His Church shall perish. "For from the rising of the sun even unto the going down of the same" the name of Jesus Christ shall be great" (Mal. 1:11).

Take hope suffering Christians. The Church of the living Lord shall yet be victorious. And then, one day, the Lord shall return, the second time, for all who believe (Heb. 9:28). The Lord will return in glory and majesty, not to disappear for seven years, and then come a third time. No, no. Jesus is coming the second time for all who believe. That is the historic faith of the

Church. It is not the Rapture Christians are to look for, but the return of Jesus in glory, and in the same manner in which He went away (Acts 1:11).

Section III:

The Rapture in Society

Chapter 6

The Rapture in Schools

My granddaughter attended a Christian school in Florida, which teaches the Rapture of the Church. Since I taught my granddaughter that the Dispensational view of the Rapture is not rooted in biblical theology, she became confused, for her teacher taught that perspective. With her in mind, I told her mother I would try to write something to help clarify the issue for a young child in elementary school. If I were teaching a Bible class on this subject, this is what I would say.

Young people, I believe that you, when properly instructed, can understand spiritual matters, and so, I want to tell you that the idea of God's people disappearing someday from the Earth is simply not taught in Scripture. Now many people disagree. Many good Christians really do believe that one day, suddenly and without warning, all over the globe, people will disappear from the earth. This event is said to be the Rapture of the Church.

It is an exciting concept. Books have been written on this topic and movies have been made. In the movies, and in the books, people who are flying on an airplane suddenly disappear.

Maybe even the pilot. Families are riding down the road, and suddenly the mother, or the father, or the children disappear. One moment they are here, and life is normal, suddenly, people are gone. It is an exciting idea. But the question remains, "Why do these people believe in the Rapture?"

Those who believe in the Rapture of the Church might say they believe the Rapture is taught in Scripture. The passage cited most often for support is 1 Thessalonians 4:16–18. So, I want you to turn to that passage, and let us read it together. The Bible says, "For the Lord himself shall descend from heaven with a shout, with the voice of the archangel, and with the trump of God: and the dead in Christ shall rise first: Then we which are alive and remain shall be caught up together with them in the clouds, to meet the Lord in the air: and so shall we ever be with the Lord. Wherefore comfort one another with these words."

Those who believe in the Rapture believe that the words "shall be caught up together with them in the clouds, to meet the Lord in the air" is the Rapture.

According to Dispensational teachers, when the Rapture takes place, people disappear, the world is left to enter into a terrible tribulation period that will last for seven years, and then at the end of that period all the Christians who left in the Rapture will return with Jesus and other saints to earth.

Now, I want you to see that 1 Thessalonians does not say anything about a seven-year tribulation period. It does not say anything about people returning in seven years. It does not say anything about people disappearing to heaven.

What the Bible does say is that when Jesus comes again there are Christians who will rise to greet Him in the air. That is what the word "meet" means in verse 17. The word refers to a friendly encounter.

Now, young people, you are familiar with this word and what it means. If the president of the United States were to come and visit your school, he would probably land at the Orlando airport. He is coming to see you. And what would you do? You would want to go and meet him, to greet him, to welcome him in a friendly encounter. Then what would happen? You would return with the president to his intended place of his travels, your school.

That is what the Bible teaches. When Jesus comes, some will go to meet Him. They will greet Him, and then escort Him to where Jesus is coming which is back to earth, the second time, for all who believe, according to the promise of Hebrews 9:28. Turn to Hebrews 9:28 in your Bible and let us read the text together. "So Christ was once offered to bear the sins of many; and unto them that look for him shall he appear the second time without sin unto salvation."

Notice that Jesus is coming the "second time." Young people, the idea of the Rapture, as taught by Dispensational teachers, creates a third coming of Jesus, and that is contrary to what we just read.

It is true. Notice that Jesus came the first time more than 2000 years ago in the virgin birth. Then, according to Dispensational teachers, He will come at the Rapture, and then, seven years later he will return a third time. First Advent (Virgin Birth), Rapture, and then the Second Coming. That is *three* comings of Christ. But the Bible says Jesus is only coming "the second time."

There is something else. The Dispensational teachers say that Jesus is coming so suddenly, people will not know what is happening. One author has called the Rapture, "The Great Snatch." It is interesting that a secret, silent coming of Christ is appealed to from one of the nosiest passage in the Bible, for in 1 Thessalonians we have "a shout, with the voice of the archangel, and with the trump of God." Now when someone shouts and blows a trumpet loud enough for the whole world to hear, well, that is not much of a secret, silent coming, to snatch people away.

The truth of the matter is that Jesus will return, not in secret, only to disappear, but He will come in the same manner, or way in which He went away.

Young people, how did Jesus go away?

We find the answer in Acts 1:9–11. Turn there in your Bibles and let us read the words of the text together. "And when he had spoken these things, while they beheld, he was taken up; and a cloud received him out of their sight. And while they looked steadfastly toward heaven as he went up, behold, two men stood by them in white apparel; Which also said, Ye men of Galilee, why stand ye gazing up into heaven? This same Jesus, which is taken up from you into heaven, shall so come in like manner as ye have seen him go into heaven."

Jesus went away, slowly, bodily, and visibly. The disciples watched in amazement as Jesus ascended, and those who will one day greet Jesus shall watch His descent. Jesus is coming again the same way, or, "in like manner," as He went away.

So, what have we learned based on what we have read in the Bible?

- We have learned that Jesus is coming the second time for all who believe.
- We have learned that some will go to meet, or greet the Lord in a friendly encounter.
- We have learned that Jesus will come with a shout, and the blast of a trumpet.
- We have learned that Jesus will descend slowly, bodily, and visibly.
- We have learned that many people are reading into the Bible some ideas that are simply not there.

There is much more that could be said on this topic, but that is our lesson for today. Let us pray, and say with the apostle John, "Even so come quickly, Lord Jesus. Amen."

Chapter 7

The Rapture in Cinema

I am tempted to adhere to an old adage, "If you cannot say something nice, do not say anything at all." I do want to say something nice about the film Final: The Rapture. I believe those who star in the film are sincere, and well meaning. I am sure that all involved in this film project believe the message they are promoting. And, I understand the purpose of the film is to win people to Jesus Christ.

But there are some objections I have to this film, beginning with the disjointed scenes. The movie purports to follow the lives of four individuals, and their reaction to the Rapture.

For those who are not familiar with Christian Dispensational Theology, the Rapture is believed to be the time when Christians suddenly disappear, by the millions, in a single day, and in a brief moment of time. Planes crash because pilots are suddenly raptured, or caught up in the air, and disappear, to heaven. Cars crash as drivers disappear, causing massive disruption in transportation. Panic and fear sets in as loved ones are gone forever. Multitudes from every walk of life, rich and poor, young and old, intellectuals and the uneducated have been raptured because of their faith in Jesus Christ. It is a sensational concept.

The *Orlando Sentinel* calls this film a "Christian horror film." The film does try to scare the audience. Conceptionally, I am not opposed to such an approach. I would rather try to scare someone into heaven, than to laugh a person into hell.

With that being said, let it be known that the movie is hard to follow. The storyline tries to trace the lives of four individuals who are left behind at the Rapture. That is not easy to do because first one character, and then another, has a flash back, each one time and again, causing great confusion as to the person and the time under consideration.

If that is not frustrating enough, a large portion of the dialogue is printed on the screen. Unless the audience knows English, Spanish, and Japanese, having to read the dialogue will take the eyes away from the action. Reading most of a movie's script is not the best way to enjoy a film, in my opinion.

I will spare making a lot of comments about the acting in the film, other than to say that much of it, no, most of it, from start to finish, by any objective standard, is silly and immature. The acting is painful to watch.

But my greatest objection to the movie is that it is essentially unbiblical. It is a movie that should never have been made, because it is presenting a theory as the true Word of God. It is not.

The theory of the Rapture of millions of people, leaving the rest of humanity to endure seven years of great tribulation under the rule and reign of an Antichrist, is simply not part of the historic Christian faith. The concept of the Rapture is not found in any of the Creeds of Christendom. It was never discussed in any Church Council. The Rapture is not part of any historic Confession of Faith, such as the Westminster Confession of Faith or the London Baptist Confession of 1689.

Until around 1830 the world had never heard of the Rapture, and for good reason. There is not a single text in the Bible that plainly teaches the Rapture of the Church, let alone a seven-year tribulation period. In the movie, several passages from the Bible are alluded to, but the audience is never allowed to read any text from Scripture. For those who are familiar with Dispensational Teaching and methodology this is not surprising.

When the Bible is opened, when the historic faith of the Christian Church is faithfully taught, it can immediately be seen that the Bible teaches that Jesus will come again to earth the second time for all who believe.

Hebrews 9:28 So Christ was once offered to bear the sins of many; and unto them that look for him shall he appear the second time without sin unto salvation.

The Rapture theory injects a third coming of Christ into Church dogma. Consider:

(1st) (2nd) (3rd)
The First Advent (Virgin Birth) + Rapture + Second Advent = Three comings of Christ.

There is something else. The Bible teaches that Christ will return in the same manner in which He went away. After His resurrection Jesus met with His disciples. The disciples had a question for Jesus which He answered, and then began His ascension into heaven. The story is told in Acts 1. "When they therefore were come together, they asked of him, saying, Lord, wilt thou at this time restore again the kingdom to Israel? And he said unto them, It is not for you to know the times or the seasons, which the Father hath put in his own power. But ye shall receive power, after that the Holy Ghost is come upon you: and ye shall be witnesses unto me both in Jerusalem, and in all Judaea, and in Samaria, and unto the uttermost part of the earth. And when he had spoken these things, while they beheld, he was taken up; and a cloud received him out of their sight. And while they looked steadfastly toward heaven as he went up, behold, two men stood by them in white apparel; Which also said, Ye men of Galilee, why stand ye gazing up into heaven? this same Jesus, which is taken up from you into heaven, shall so come in like manner as ye have seen him go into heaven."

As the Rapture theory is presented, as the movie portrays this unbiblical and unhistorical teaching, Jesus does not return slowly and visibly to earth in the same manner as He went away. Rather, Jesus comes suddenly, and disappears with millions in the blink of an eye. In contrast, the Bible says, "Behold, he cometh with clouds; and every eye shall see him, and they also which pierced him: and all kindreds of the earth shall wail because of him. Even so, Amen" (Rev. 1:7).

In the movie, people are given a second chance to repent, and believe in Christ and be saved. That is not a biblical concept. When Jesus Comes the second time for all who believe the lost will be confirmed in their unbelief. The Bible teaches that now is the time to repent and trust Christ as Savior. "For he says, 'In the time of my favor I heard you, and in the day of salvation I helped you.' I tell you, now is the time of God's favor, now is the day of salvation" (2 Cor. 6:2 NIV).

Let the truth of God's Word go forth: today is the day of salvation. There will be no second chance. "See to it, brothers, that none of you has a sinful, unbelieving heart that turns away from the living God. But encourage one another daily, as long as it is called Today, so that none of you may be hardened by sin's deceitfulness. We have come to share in Christ if we hold firmly till the end the confidence we had at first. As has just been said: 'Today, if you hear his voice, do not harden your hearts as you did in the rebellion'" (Heb. 3:12–15 NIV).

When Jesus comes, individuals who have rejected Him will be confirmed in their sin. There will be no second chance to repent and be saved as the movie teaches. In contrast to the movie, in contrast to The System known as Dispensationalism, read the Scriptures, and tremble if you are an unbeliever.

> Let him who does wrong continue to do wrong; let him who is vile continue to be vile; let him who does right continue to do right; and let him who is holy continue to be holy. Behold, I am coming soon! My reward is with me, and I will give to everyone according to what he has

done. I am the Alpha and the Omega, the First and the Last, the Beginning and the End. Blessed are those who wash their robes, that they may have the right to the tree of life and may go through the gates into the city. Outside are the dogs, those who practice magic arts, the sexually immoral, the murderers, the idolaters and everyone who loves and practices falsehood. I, Jesus, have sent my angel to give you this testimony for the Churches. I am the Root and the Offspring of David, and the bright Morning Star. The Spirit and the bride say, "Come!" And let him who hears say, "Come!" Whoever is thirsty, let him come; and whoever wishes, let him take the free gift of the water of life. I warn everyone who hears the words of the prophecy of this book: If anyone adds anything to them, God will add to him the plagues described in this book. And if anyone takes words away from this book of prophecy, God will take away from him his share in the tree of life and in the holy city, which are described in this book. He who testifies to these things says, "Yes, I am coming soon." Amen. Come, Lord Jesus. The grace of the Lord Jesus be with God's people. Amen (Rev. 22:11–21 NIV).

My heart goes out to those who make Christian movies, because it is right and proper that believers be involved in all the arts and sciences. But what is portrayed on film must be biblical, or, in the end more harm will be done than good. Teaching individuals that they will have a second chance to be saved is one great harm that this movie, and the Rapture theory, perpetuates. May God forgive all who are doing this in ignorance.

I would love to see a movie produced about the true Second Coming of Jesus Christ, but only as it is taught in Scripture. That would be a movie worth supporting by all Christians.

Chapter 8

The Last Day of Human History

"And as it is appointed unto men once to die, but after this the judgment: So Christ was once offered to bear the sins of many; and unto them that look for Him shall He appear the second time without sin unto salvation" (Heb. 9:27–28).

When Adam first opened his eyes on the day of his creation, he awakened to a world of awesome beauty. It was a perfect world that Adam would trod. It was the original temple built by God.

> His fiat laid the cornerstone,
>   And heaved its pillars, one by one,
> He hung its starry roof on high,
>   The broad, illimitable [expansive] sky;
> He spread its pavement, green and light,
>   And curtained it with morning light.
> The mountains in their places stood,
>   The sea, the sky, and "all was good,"
> And when its first pure praise rang
>   The morning stars together sang.   —Nathanial P. Willis

The angels would not sing for long, nor would Adam enjoy the beauties of the earth, for sin soon found its way into Paradise. With sin came a curse upon all creation. Death began to stalk the universe. Thorns appeared, and animals suddenly turned one upon another until nature was blood red in tooth and claw. Paradise was lost. "Wherefore, as by one man sin entered into the world, and death by sin" (Rom. 5:12).

Today, modern science is a reluctant witness to the spiritual judgment that came into the world. Science confirms that the universe is dying according to the Second Law of Thermodynamics, which is the Law of Entropy. This Law states that all forms go from order to disorder. The Universe is dying. Unless something happens, the sun will one day cease to shine, and the stars will no longer twinkle. The hour is coming when the moon will refuse to reflect light. One day the grass will not be able to grow.

One day, animals will no longer find food to eat. One day, life on planet earth will be silent for the globe will be wrapped in ice and darkness. Such is the future of the heavens and the earth, apart from Divine intervention. But all of these events shall never happen, because God has already revealed that the day will come when He will make a new heaven and a new earth. There will be a time when human history will end, and eternal history will begin. While we live in this present period, we wait for the age to come wherein dwelleth righteousness. The new age will begin on the day that history ends.

The history of mankind is a very interesting chronicle. It is like a great memoir, talking about the rise and fall of magnificent and majestic empires. The history of mankind is like a compelling drama, full of interesting characters that play their parts on the stage of life.

The history of mankind is like an epic poem. There is travel and intrigue, and much adventure. But when the tale is told, the poem is placed back on the dusty shelf of forgetfulness. The history of mankind is very interesting, but it will one day end.

Many people thought that history would initially end on March 21, 1843, based upon the prophetic teachings of William Miller, of New England.

Many people thought that history would literally end on October 28, 1962. The United States intelligence community had discovered the existence of Soviet supplied missile installations in Cuba. U-2 photo flights confirmed that the silos for offensive weapons had been built, and that the nuclear warheads were on their way from Russia.

President Kennedy decided that a naval blockade of the island might prevent the shipments of arms from reaching Cuba. But what would happen if the Russian ships refused to recognize the arbitrary blockade boundaries in international waters? What would happen if the Russians tried to run the blockade and American ships were fired upon?

The world waited and watched while wondering what Soviet premier Nikita Khrushchev would do. College students debated among themselves if they should study for their exams on Monday. There would be no exams on Monday if a nuclear war started between the two great super-powers. There might be no United States. In the end, Khrushchev blinked. He backed down. He agreed to remove the arsenal of mass destruction, and the world breathed a sigh of relief.

History did not come to an end in October of 1962. But it will end someday. When shall that day arrive? No one knows, and no one can accurately predict it though many have tried and are still trying. Despite all of the failed prophecies, and despite all of the false modern-day prophets found in religious circles, the day is coming when Jesus Christ will appear the second time for all who believe. And when Jesus comes, it will be the last day of human history, as we know it. Eternal history will begin.

Regarding the day of the Lord's appearance, when the great transaction is made from the temporal to the eternal, there are some details provided in the Bible as to what will happen.

The last day of history will begin like all other days. The sun will rise, and the birds will begin to sing. People will get up, get dressed, eat breakfast, and go off to work or play, never suspecting that in just a few hours the universe itself will be forever changed. Somewhere, a young woman will awaken expecting to be married before the sun sets. Somewhere, a businessman will dream of concluding a major agreement with a giant corporation. Somewhere, a party will be planned. It is hoped that there will be eating and drinking and much laughter.

The day will progress as normal, until suddenly, the word spreads throughout the world from mouth to mouth and from ear to ear, "Something supernatural is taking place." "Look up in the sky!" People will turn their eyes towards the heavens and gasp with alarm. It is a supernatural invasion. There is a mass movement of something from outer space. It is entering this atmosphere and moving towards earth. Slowly, deliberating, something or Someone, is coming to earth. "What does it all mean?" Millions will wonder in alarm.

Initially, most of humanity will not know what is taking place on this last day of history, but the Church will know. This is nothing less than the promise of the angels being fulfilled as spoken to a small group of startled men on a hilltop outside the city of Jerusalem more than two thousand years ago. There, the disciples of Jesus Christ were told that their Lord and Saviour would return to earth in the manner in which He left. The angels had said, "Ye men of Galilee, why stand ye gazing up into heaven? This same Jesus, which is taken up from you into heaven, shall so come in like manner as ye have seen Him go into heaven" (Acts 1:11).

Upon reflection, the disciples remembered that Jesus had said to them in quiet serenity, "Let not your hearts be troubled. In my Father's house are many mansion, if it were not so I would have told you. I go to prepare a place for you; that where I am there ye may be also" (John 14:1).

So Jesus went to heaven following His resurrection, and the angels sang as they welcomed Him home. When Fredrick Handel was writing his great masterpiece The Messiah, he considered the ascension of Christ into heaven. He imagined that the angels sang together the words of Psalm 24:7–10 as they welcomed Jesus back home. There was a shout in the celestial sky as the angels cried,

> Lift up your heads, O ye gates;
>> And be lifted up, ye everlasting doors;
>
> And the King of Glory will come in.

The angels at the gates of heaven, when they heard the other angels singing, "Lift up your heads, O ye gates," answered, "Who is the King of Glory?"

The angels who were accompanying Jesus replied:

> The Lord strong and mighty,
>> The Lord strong and mighty
>
> The Lord mighty in battle.

Then the angels who were accompanying Jesus to His Father's home wished to have the gates opened wide to receive Him, and so again they sang out in triumphant challenge,

> Lift up your heads, O ye gates;
>> And be ye lifted up, ye everlasting doors;
>
> And the King of Glory will come in."

Again the angels by the gates of heaven sang out with joy and gladness:

> Who is the King of Glory?
>> Who is the King of Glory?

The angels who were with Jesus replied in an ever increasing swell of assurance,

> The Lord of Hosts,
> The Lord of Hosts,
> He is the King of Glory,
> He is the King of Glory!

Then the angels who kept the heavenly entrance opened wide the gates, and Jesus, the King of Glory passed through them into His Father's home. To welcome Him, all the hosts of heaven continued to sing a song of praise—the angels that were with Jesus and the angels that were by the gates, and the angels who were around the throne of God all sang praises to Jesus, the Friend and Redeemer of mankind. The wonderful song they sang declared,

> And He shall reign forever and ever.
> King of kings, and Lord of lords.
> Hallelujah! Hallelujah!
> Hallelujah! Hallelujah!

But Jesus never meant to stay in heaven. It was, and is, His stated intention to return to earth to gather His Bride unto Himself at the end of time. On the last day of history the promise of Christ to return to His Church will be kept. "For the Lord Himself shall descend from heaven with a shout, with the voice of the arch-angel, and with the trump of God" (1 Thess. 4:16).

As the Lord descends from heaven with the loud blast of the heavenly trumpet and the voice of the archangel, the Bible says that Christians on earth will rise to meet the Lord in the air.

The word "meet" is a very important word. In the original it is *apuntesis* [ap-an'-tay-sis] and refers to a friendly encounter. The special idea of the word was the official welcome of a newly arrived dignitary (Moulton, *Greek Testament Grammar*, Vol. 1, p. 14). This word is used elsewhere in scripture. It is used in Matthew 25:1, 6 and in Acts 28:14–16.

In each place the concept is that people went out to "meet" someone only to escort that person back to the very place where he was coming to.

> Then shall the kingdom of heaven be likened unto ten virgins, which took their lamps, and went forth to meet [greet] the bridegroom (Matt. 25:1).
>
> And at midnight there was a cry made, Behold, the bridegroom cometh; go ye out to meet [greet] him (Matt. 25:6).
>
> Where we found brethren, and were desired to tarry with them seven days: and so we went toward Rome. And from thence, when the brethren heard of us, they came to meet [greet] us as far as Appii forum, and the three taverns: whom when Paul saw, he thanked God, and took courage. And when we came to Rome, the centurion delivered the prisoners to the captain of the guard: but Paul was suffered to dwell by himself with a soldier that kept him (Acts 28:14–16).

The Christians will one day rise to meet the coming King of kings as He returns the second time for all who believe (Heb. 9:28). Christians will welcome the Lord and escort Him back to earth.

As the heavenly host, led by the glorified, resurrected Christ continues to move to Earth, men and women and young people who are not Christian and who are not converted will begin to be afraid. They already know what this Second Coming of Christ means for them. The gospel of the Kingdom will have been preached in all the world for a witness unto all nations (Matt. 24:14). No one will be without excuse as Christ comes looking for faith on the earth. This is the day of final judgment for multitudes, and they know it.

This is the day spoken of by Enoch, "the seventh from Adam who prophesied saying, Behold, the Lord cometh with ten thousand of His saints, To execute judgment upon all, and to convince all that are ungodly among them of their ungodly deeds which they have ungodly committed, and of all their hard speeches which ungodly sinners have spoken against Him" (Jude 1:14–15).

When Jesus Christ returns in the brightness of His glory with the angels of God and the saints of the ages, He will have a specific place that He will visit. While countless cameras record His advent and satellites follow His every movement, the Lord Jesus will make His way toward the ancient, City of Peace. Jesus will return to the Holy Land.

On that day His feet will touch the Mount of Olives, which is before Jerusalem on the East. "And his feet shall stand in that day upon the mount of Olives, which is before Jerusalem on the east, and the mount of Olives shall cleave in the midst thereof toward the east and toward the west, and there shall be a very great valley;

and half of the mountain shall remove toward the north, and half of it toward the south" (Zech. 14:4).

The Lord will yet stand again on the Mount of Olives, despite resistance to His coming on that day. One personage who will not want the Lord to reach earth, and Palestine is the Man of Sin who is the Son of Perdition. He knows that he will be charged with specific sins by the Savior, for it is he, "Who opposeth and exalteth Himself above all that is called God, or that is worshiped; so that He as God sitteth in the Temple of God, showing Himself that He is God" (2 Thess. 2:4).

Now God in Christ Jesus has returned to expose the "Wicked One, whose coming is after the working of Satan with all power and signs and lying wonders, And with all deceivableness of unrighteousness in them that perish; because they received not the love of the truth, that they might be saved" (2 Thess. 2:9–10).

When Jesus comes He shall, "consume with the Spirit of His mouth, and shall destroy with the brightness of His coming" the Man of Sin and his followers (2 Thess. 2:8). Those who have ignored the Lord, can ignore Him no longer. He has returned. Those who have blasphemed His holy name will cease to curse. He has returned. The blasphemies of the wicked will be turned into prayers, but the prayers will be unreasonable as individuals plead with the mountains saying, "Fall on us, and hide us from the face of Him that sitteth on the throne, and from the wrath of the Lamb. For the great day of His wrath is come; and who shall be able to stand" (Rev. 6:16–17).

But the mountains will not fall on the ungodly on the Last Day, for the Last Day is also the Day of Judgment in which no one can hide. Even those who are in the grave will not be safe for the hour has come, "in the which all that are in the graves shall hear His voice, And shall come forth; they that have done good, unto the resurrection of life; and they that have done evil, unto the resurrection of damnation" (John 5:28–29). The damnation of the wicked shall be according to Divine justice. On the Last Day the Lord of Righteousness will say to all those who have rejected Him,

> Ye call Me Master and obey Me not,
> Ye call Me Light and see Me not,
> Ye call Me Way and walk not,
> Ye call Me Life and desire Me not,
>
> Ye call Me Wise and follow Me not,
> Ye call Me Fair and love Me not,
> Ye call Me Rich and ask Me not,
> Ye call Me Eternal and seek Me not,
> Ye call Me Gracious and trust Me not,
> Ye call Me Noble and serve Me not,
> Ye call Me Mighty and honor Me not,
> Ye call Me Just and fear Me not;
> If I condemn you, blame Me not.
>
> —Source Unknown

While the wicked fight, and cry, and tremble, and are carried away like Judas unto their own place, the experience of the Church will be far different. On the Last Day, the Church will be rejoicing. This is the day for which the Church has long prayed, "Even so come quickly, Lord Jesus."

This is the day of the Marriage Supper of the Lamb. The Bridegroom has come for his Bride whom He sees as altogether lovely without spot or wrinkle (Eph. 5:27). It would make the Bride to blush if some were to hear the words from her Lord that she keeps next to her heart. She has heard His voice already and she longs to hear it again. The Church waits for the Bridegroom to come and whisper once more the things He has already said in the Song of Solomon.

> How beautiful you are, my darling! Oh, how beautiful.
> Your voice is sweet, and your face is lovely.
> Like a lily among thorns is my darling among the maidens.
> How delightful is your love . . .
> How much more pleasing is your love than wine.
> You have stolen my heart.
> The King is held captive (Song 1:15; 2:14; 2:2; 4:10; 8:4).

The spiritual truth is that the beauty of His Bride enchants the coming King. Did He not die for her? Does He not ever live to intercede for her? Did He not promise that He would return for her? Is love for her not the all-consuming passion of the Messiah's march to victory? "Listen, O daughter, consider and give your ear: Forget your people and your father's house. The King is enthralled by your beauty; honor Him, for He is your Lord" (Ps. 45:10).

As the bride looks forward to the day of her marriage, so the Church can look forward to The Last Day; it is the day of her eternal union with Christ in a glorified body. On the Last Day of history, those who have died in Christ will receive a resurrected body as they come with Him; and those on earth who love the Lord will be changed. "Behold, I shew you a mystery; We shall not all sleep, but we shall all be changed, In a moment, in the twinkling of an eye, at the last trump: for the trumpet shall sound, and the dead shall be raised incorruptible, and we shall be changed" (1 Cor. 15:51–52).

Because these things are true according to Scripture, it is wise for all men to prepare for The Last Day of history Divine preparation is made when Christ is received as Lord and Savior, and life is lived for His honor and His glory. If tomorrow were The Last Day of human history, would you be numbered with those who would resist His arrival, or would your heart be rejoicing while saying to others,

> Marvelous messages we bring,
> Glorious carol we sing,
> Wonderful word of the King!
> Jesus is coming again!

The Bible teaches that there is a special crown for all who love the appearance of Christ. "Henceforth there is laid up for me a crown of righteousness, which the Lord, the righteous judge, shall give me at that day: and not to me only, but unto all them also that love his appearing" (2 Tim. 4:8). Do you love the appearance of Christ? Do you long for His Second Coming? As you look toward the heavens, will your heart be able to sing on the last day of human history,

> O the King is coming, The King is coming!
> I just heard the trumpets sounding,
> And now His face I see;
> O the King is coming, the King is coming!
> Praise God, He's coming for me!
> —Gloria and Bill Gaither and Charles Millhuff

Come to Christ. Love Him with all of your heart, and He will come for you on the last day of human history.

Section IV:

The Rapture in Doctrinal Review

Chapter 9

Rapture Mania

The Six Raptures of Scripture

It has been suggested by various Dispensational teachers that there are no less than six raptures taught in Scripture. If the Latin term, "rapture," is used in a literal, narrow sense meaning "to take," "to seize," "to snatch," "to translate," "to ascend," "to be caught up"; if the term is made to be synonymous with its parallel English (rapture), Greek (*harpazō*), Hebrew (*laqach*), then the following "raptures" can be found in Scripture.

- The rapture of Enoch
- The rapture of Elijah
- The rapture of Jesus
- The rapture of Philip
- The rapture of believers in Christ
- The rapture of the Two Witnesses of Revelation

The rapture of Enoch is based on a passage in the book of Hebrews, commenting on a passage in Genesis 5. "By faith Enoch was translated that he should not see death; and was not found, because God had translated him: for before his translation he had this testimony, that he pleased God" (Heb. 11:5).

A Dispensational reading of this passage would be: "By faith Enoch was raptured that he should not see death; and was not found, because God had translated him: for before his translation he had this testimony, that he pleased God." The Bible says, "And Enoch walked with God: and he was not; for God took him" (Gen. 5:24). A Dispensational reading of this passage would be: "And Enoch walked with God: and he was not; for God raptured him."

The Greek word for "translated" in Hebrews 11:5 is *metastrephō*, to turn across, i.e., transmute or (figuratively) corrupt. It is translated in the KJV, *pervert*, and *turn*.

The Hebrew word for "took" in Genesis 5:24 is *laqach*, to take (in the widest variety of applications): KJV, accept, bring, buy, carry away, drawn, fetch, get, enfold, many, mingle, place, receive (-ing), reserve, seize, send for, take (away, -ing, up), use, win. The author of Hebrews focuses attention upon the faith of Enoch, not his typology. Prior to his translation, Enoch's faith pleased God. Matthew Henry observes, "Those who by faith walk with God in a sinful world are pleasing to him, and he will give them marks of his favor, and put honour upon them."

The rapture of Elijah is found in 2 Kings 2:11. We read that Elijah went up by a whirlwind into heaven. "And it came to pass, as they still went on, and talked, that, behold, there appeared a chariot of fire, and horses of fire, and parted them both asunder; and Elijah went up by a whirlwind into heaven" (2 Kgs. 2:11).

A Dispensational reading of this passage would be: And it came to pass, as they still went on, and talked, that, behold, there appeared a chariot of fire, and horses of fire, and parted them both asunder; and Elijah was raptured by a whirlwind into heaven. The words "went up," translate the Hebrew word, 'alah (aw-law'); to ascend.

Much speculation is associated with the translation of Enoch and Elijah. The words of John Calvin are worthy of remembrance. Commenting on Hebrews 11:5, Calvin wrote:

> As to the subtle questions which the curious usually moot, it is better to pass them over, without taking much notice of them. They ask, what became of these two men, Enoch and Elijah? And then, that they may not appear merely to ask questions, they imagine that they are reserved for the last days of the Church, that they may then come forth into the world; and for this purpose, the Revelation of John is referred to. Let us leave this airy philosophy to those light and vain minds, which cannot be satisfied with what is solid. Let it suffice us to know, that their translation was a sort of extraordinary death; nor let us doubt but that they were divested of their mortal and corruptible flesh, in order that they might, with the other members of Christ, be renewed into a blessed immortality. (*Commentary on Hebrews*)

Once speculation begins, once the imagination is let loose on Scripture, once freedom is found to read meaning *into* Scripture something not warranted, there is no end to what might be conjured up. If Enoch is a type of the Church, then maybe Elijah is a type of the Church, which can look forward to going to heaven in a chariot! Why not? Who is to say otherwise?

Moving from the rapture of Enoch, and the rapture of Elijah, attention can be given to the rapture of Jesus, based on a passage in the Revelation. "And she brought forth a man child, who was to rule all nations with a rod of iron: and her child was caught up unto God, and to his throne" (Rev. 12:5).

A Dispensational reading of this passage would be: "And she brought forth a man child, who was to rule all nations with a rod of iron: and her child was raptured unto God, and to his throne."

Historically, the Church has referred to the return of Christ to heaven, as His ascension.

> And when he had spoken these things, while they beheld, he was taken up; and a cloud received him out of their sight. And while they looked steadfastly toward heaven as he went up, behold, two men stood by them in white apparel; Which also said, Ye men of Galilee, why stand ye gazing up into heaven? This same Jesus, which is taken up from you into heaven, shall so come in like manner as ye have seen him go into heaven (Acts 1:9–11).

The word for "caught up" is the same Greek word, *harpazō*, that is found in 1 Thessalonians 4:17. "Then we who are alive and remain shall be caught up [*harpazō*] together with them in the clouds to meet the Lord in the air. And thus we shall always be with the Lord" (1 Thess. 4:17).

The next rapture seen in Scripture is that of Philip who was caught up after speaking with the eunuch. "And when they were come up out of the water, the Spirit of the Lord caught away Philip, that the eunuch saw him no more: and he went on his way rejoicing" (Acts 8:39).

A Dispensational reading of this passage would be: "And when they were come up out of the water, the Spirit of the Lord raptured Philip, that the eunuch saw him no more: and he went on his way rejoicing."

Later, Philip was found preaching at Azotus (Acts 8:40). If Philip is seen as a type of the Church, then Christians might be able to have their own personal raptures around town. Who is to say otherwise?

Another rapture is seen in Revelation 11, when the two witnesses are taken up: "And after three days and an half the Spirit of life from God entered into them, and they stood upon their feet; and great fear fell upon them which saw them. And they heard a great voice from heaven saying unto them, Come up hither. And they ascended up to heaven in a cloud; and their enemies beheld them" (Rev. 11:11–12).

A Dispensational reading of this passage would be: "And after three days and an half the Spirit of life from God entered into them, and they stood upon their feet; and great fear fell upon them which saw them. And they heard a great voice from heaven saying unto them, Come up hither. And they were raptured to heaven in a cloud; and their enemies beheld them."

According to Dispensational theology, this rapture of the two witnesses takes place during the great tribulation period of seven years, so perhaps it should be taught that there is going to be a rapture after Jesus raptures the Church, which is said to have occurred prior to the great tribulation. Who is to say otherwise?

Finally, there is the rapture where believers will be taken up to meet Christ.

"Then we which are alive and remain shall be caught up together with them in the clouds, to meet the Lord in the air: and so shall we ever be with the Lord" (1 Thess. 4:17).

There are three practical problems when discussing the concept of the rapture.

One practical problem, is that the literal meaning of the Latin term, *raptura*, the Greek term, *harpazō*, the Hebrew term, *laqach*, or the English word, rapture, has been confiscated by Dispensational theology and its meaning changed. This happens in society. The word "gay," when used in the 1920s, means something far different in today's vernacular. The English usage of the word *rapture* is especially problematic, because the term is given a theological meaning that goes beyond simply being "taken," "translated," "carried away," "seized," or "caught up."

To a devout Dispensationalist, the word rapture is to be capitalized in order to refer to a separate event that takes place seven years prior to the Second Coming of Christ. The word rapture speaks of leaving earth to go to heaven with Jesus, and then returning with Him after a period of great tribulation on earth. The word speaks of escapism. The Church was damaged historically, when, in the Apostle's Creed, the affirmation of faith, "I believe in the holy catholic Church," was changed to, "I believe in the holy Catholic Church," meaning the Church of Rome. The change from a little "c" to a capital "C," changed the meaning of the word "catholic" (literally, universal).

A second practical problem, when discussing the concept of the rapture, is that Church history is dismissed, the Creeds of Christendom are ignored, and the Confessions of Faith are set aside, in favor of a sensational, and novel, teaching of the nineteenth century that has no roots in the historic faith of the Church. However, it is the apostolic faith, the historic faith, which saints are to contend for. "Beloved, when I gave all diligence to write unto you of the common salvation, it was needful for me to write unto you, and exhort you that ye should earnestly contend for the faith which was once delivered unto the saints" (Jude 3).

A third practical problem, when discussing the concept of the rapture, is that people are emotionally attached to what they have learned. It is hard to listen to any teaching that challenges, or changes, what a person is familiar with. Sometimes, renewed attention should be given to the historic faith of the Church, the simplicity of Scripture, and the whole counsel of God. "Wherefore, my beloved brethren, let every man be swift to hear, slow to speak, slow to wrath" (Jas. 1:19).

Chapter 10

The System

The word *rapture* is not found in the New Testament. That bears repeating. Rapture, the noun, is not found in Scripture. However, the idea conveyed in the word is plainly scriptural, when properly understood. For example, when Paul speaks in 1 Thessalonians 4 about individuals being caught up to meet him, meet the Lord in the air, he talking about a rapture.

> For the Lord himself shall descend from heaven with a shout, with the voice of the archangel, and with the trump of God: and the dead in Christ shall rise first: Then we which are alive and remain shall be caught up together with them in the clouds, to meet the Lord in the air: and so, shall we ever be with the Lord. Wherefore comfort one another with these words" (1 Thess. 4:16–18).

The term that is used, is a term which is rendered in the Latin vulgate by the Latin word *rapiō* which means "to seize or to catch." And it's the word from which we get, rapture by way of the Latin verb, *rapiō*. It is not wrong to take the term as being a biblical term, though the word itself is not mentioned.

The Scriptures

It is not uncommon for those who teach Dispensational theology, and the Rapture theory, to dismiss those who disagree with them as being "ignorant." That is an ad hominem approach which is an appeal to personal considerations rather than an argument. It is on the level of the preacher who put in the margin of his notes on a text he was preaching from, "Shout here, weak point."

The truth of the matter is that multitudes of competent Greek scholars, such as Dr. R. C. Sproul, reject the teaching of the Rapture on grammatical, historical, and logical grounds.

Grammatical Grounds. The word "meet" in 1 Thessalonians 4:17 is a very important word. The word is *apantesis* (ap-an'-tay-sis) and refers to "a (friendly) encounter." When the King of king returns to earth the second time for all who believe (Heb. 9:28), He should be met.

Historical Grounds. There is nothing in the text that says the Church will meet the Lord and disappear for seven years. That is the fabrication of Dispensational teaching, and is not found in any historic creed of Christendom, nor has this novel doctrine been discussed at any Church council. There is good reason. None of the Church Fathers thought of the Rapture, nor did any of the Reformers, many of whom were brilliant Greek and Hebrew scholars.

Logical Grounds. The Rapture theory introduces a *third* coming into Christian eschatology.

First Coming	Second Coming	Third Coming
The Virgin Birth	The Rapture	The Second Advent

Because the Rapture theory teaches a secret, silent coming of Christ, this aberrant teaching must be challenged by Scripture.

First, the only "secret" coming of Christ talked about in Scripture was spoken of by Christ, and His counsel was, "believe it not!"

> Then if any man shall say unto you, Lo, here is Christ, or there; believe it not. For there shall arise false Christs, and false prophets, and shall shew great signs and wonders; insomuch that, if it were possible, they shall deceive the very elect. Behold, I have told you before. Wherefore if they shall say unto you, Behold, he is in the desert; go not forth: behold, he is in the secret chambers; believe it not" (Matt. 24:23–26).

Second, the angels said that Jesus would return in the same manner in which He went away, slowly, visibly, and bodily – but not secretly or suddenly. "Which also said, Ye men of Galilee, why stand ye gazing up into heaven? This same Jesus, which is taken up from you into heaven, shall so come in like manner as ye have seen him go into heaven" (Acts 1:11).

Third, the Bible says Christ will return the second time, not in stages or phases, but the second time for all that believe. "So, Christ was once offered to bear the sins of many; and unto them that look for him shall he appear the second time without sin unto salvation" (Heb. 9:28).

In addition to teaching that the Rapture is a secret coming, The System teaches it is a silent coming, and then The System appeals to one of the noisiest passages in the Bible! There will be a shout, and the voice of the archangel.

> For this we say unto you by the word of the Lord, that we which are alive and remain unto the coming of the Lord shall not prevent them which are asleep. For the Lord himself shall descend from heaven with a shout, with the voice of the archangel, and with the trump of God: and the dead in Christ shall rise first: Then we which are alive and remain shall be caught up together with them in the clouds, to meet the Lord in the air: and so shall we ever be with the Lord. Wherefore comfort one another with these words (1 Thess. 4:15–18).

There is nothing secret, or silent, about the return of the Lord, for it is the day of the great resurrection, and the day of a great transformation of our bodies.

> Behold, I shew you a mystery; We shall not all sleep, but we shall all be changed, In a moment, in the twinkling of an eye, at the last trump: for the trumpet shall sound, and the dead shall be raised incorruptible, and we shall be changed. For this corruptible must put on incorruption, and this mortal must put on immortality. So when this corruptible shall have put on incorruption, and this mortal shall have put on immortality, then shall be brought

to pass the saying that is written, Death is swallowed up in victory. O death, where is thy sting? O grave, where is thy victory?" (1 Cor. 15:51).

Chapter 11

The Problem with the Rapture Theory

The Rapture refers to a passage in First Thessalonians 4, where Christians are "caught up" in the clouds to meet the Lord in the air.

> For this we say unto you by the word of the Lord, that we which are alive and remain unto the coming of the Lord shall not prevent them which are asleep. For the Lord himself shall descend from heaven with a shout, with the voice of the archangel, and with the trump of God: and the dead in Christ shall rise first: Then we which are alive and remain shall be caught up together with them in the clouds, to meet the Lord in the air: and so shall we ever be with the Lord. Wherefore comfort one another with these words (1 Thess. 4:15–18).

Many Christians believe that this being "caught up" to meet the Lord will occur before a Great Tribulation Period of seven years, which is still in the near future. According to the Rapture teaching, prior to the Great Tribulation, Christians will simply disappear to meet Jesus in the air, return to heaven with Him and await the end of time, which will come seven years later when everyone returns to earth with the Lord who will set up a millennium kingdom.

But notice, in 1 Thessalonians 4:15, Paul says that "... we who are alive," meaning, "we who are left behind," shall be caught up. This is a very important point to notice because those who are "left behind" get caught up to meet the Lord. The word for "meet" is the Greek word which means, "a friendly encounter." It was a moment of greeting someone coming.

In Luke 17, and in a similar passage in Matthew 24, Scripture compares the coming of the Lord to the days of Noah and the days of Lot. Matthew 24 puts it this way: "As were the days of Noah, so will be the coming of the Son of man ... [they ate, they drank, they married] and they did not know until the flood came and swept them all away, so will be the coming of the Son of man. Then two men will be in the field, one is taken and one is left. Two women grinding at the mill, one is taken one is left." "One is taken, one is left"— the Rapture, right? Jesus takes the Christians and leaves behind non-Christians. That is what The System teaches.

However, there are two fundamental problems with this interpretation. In the passages from Luke 17 and Matthew 24, Jesus' coming is compared to the days of Noah and to the days of Lot. What happened in the days of Noah? Well, after the flood, some were left behind? Who was left behind? Noah and his family, who were righteous. The unrighteous were taken and the righteous were left behind. After Sodom and Gomorrah was destroyed by fire, who was left behind? The Bible teaches that Lot and his daughters were left behind. The unrighteous were destroyed and the righteous were left behind.

Another problem with the Rapture theory is found in 1 Thessalonians 4, which says that those who are "left" get to meet Jesus in the air. Since that is a wonderful event, every Christian should want to be present in order to meet and greet Jesus as He returns.

For the third time the biblical illustration is that the unrighteous are destroyed while the righteous are left behind. In this discussion, Matthew 13:39–43 is important.

> ... and the enemy who sowed them [the bad seed] is the devil; the harvest is the close of the age, and the reapers are angels. Just as the weeds are gathered and burned with fire, so will it be at the close of the age. The Son of man will send His angels and they will gather out of His kingdom all causes of sin and all evildoers, and throw them into the furnace of fire; there men will weep and gnash their teeth. Then the righteous will shine like the sun in the kingdom of their Father.

When Scripture says that "one is taken and one is left," as it does in Luke 17 and Matthew 24, it is not talking about the Rapture, it is talking about the harvest at the close of the age. The ones, who are taken, as it says in Matthew 13, are the evildoers. The angels have taken them and tossed them into the furnace of fire.

Chapter 12

The Resurrection and the Rapture

The Preterist View

Preterism is the system of belief that the future prophesies of Matthew 24, Mark 13, and Luke 21 were fulfilled by the end of the first century of the Christian era. The term "Preterist" is taken from the Hebrew languages "Preterite" tense, which is the "past perfect" sense, in terms of once for all completion, or accomplishment.

A distinction must be made between the "Full Preterist" and the "Partial Preterist" advocates. Partial Preterist believe that the return of Jesus, the great resurrection, and a new heaven and new earth are future events. The destruction of Jerusalem in A.D. 70 was a coming of Christ, but not the coming of Christ.

While both positions of Preterism unite on many points, division takes place concerning the resurrection. In 1 Corinthians 15, Paul speaks about the resurrection.

> Now this I say, brethren, that flesh and blood cannot inherit the kingdom of God; neither doth corruption inherit incorruption. Behold, I shew you a mystery; We shall not all sleep, but we shall all be changed, In a moment, in the twinkling of an eye, at the last trump: for the trumpet shall sound, and the dead shall be raised incorruptible, and we shall be changed. For this corruptible must put on incorruption, and this mortal must put on immortality. So when this corruptible shall have put on incorruption, and this mortal shall have put on immortality, then shall be brought to pass the saying that is written, Death is swallowed up in victory. O death, where is thy sting? O grave, where is thy victory? The sting of death is sin; and the strength of sin is the law. But thanks be to God, which giveth us the victory through our Lord Jesus Christ. Therefore, my beloved brethren, be ye steadfast, unmoveable, always abounding in the work of the Lord, forasmuch as ye know that your labour is not in vain in the Lord (1 Cor. 15:50–58).

United to Scripture is the Apostles' Creed, which affirms faith in the resurrection of the body.

> I believe in God the Father Almighty, Maker of heaven and earth.
> And in Jesus Christ his only Son our Lord; who was conceived by the Holy Ghost, born of the Virgin Mary, suffered under Pontius Pilate, was crucified, dead, and buried; he descended into hell; the third day he rose again from the dead; he ascended into heaven, and

sitteth on the right hand of God the Father Almighty; from thence he shall come to judge the quick and the dead.

I believe in the Holy Ghost; the holy catholic Church; the communion of saints; the forgiveness of sins; the resurrection of the body; and the life everlasting. AMEN.

As Christ has promised to be the first fruits of those who are raised from the dead, the saints anticipate a resurrection body. The soul and body are to be forever united. The saints are not to wander in a disembodied state throughout eternity. Full Preterist argue that the resurrection has already been fulfilled in the past.

Why Do Preterist Believe This?

Turning to 1 Corinthians 15:51–52, Preterist notice that no time frame is given for the fulfillment of the text. However, they seize upon the word "we." Verse 52 says, "and we shall be changed."

The argument is that the word "we" indicates a first century fulfillment. This resurrection passage is then linked to the Rapture of 1 Thessalonians 4:17 which includes the language, "Then we which are alive . . ." Again, the argument is that Paul includes himself in the events.

Of course, the language of identity does not necessitate that Paul believed he would personally be alive at an immediate Rapture, or Resurrection. The word "we" is used in an expanded sense. Paul would be included in the resurrection whenever it took place, in the first century, or later.

The Higher Critics have seized upon the language of Paul to declare that he was mistaken in his belief that he would be part of the final coming in his generation, and a general resurrection. Therefore, the Scriptures cannot be true. However, a possible inference from a text does not necessitate that inference from the text.

In order for the Preterist position to prevail, the resurrection, and the Rapture must be spiritualized. Spiritualizing the resurrection, and the Rapture, is not easy to do contextually, because the language of Scripture is plainly dealing with literal and bodily events.

It is difficult to spiritualize the bodily resurrection of the saints, without, at the same time, denying the bodily resurrection of the saints. If the resurrection is only spiritual, then it is manifestly not a physical resurrection.

Preterism has been charged with Gnosticism, which also denied the resurrection of Jesus.

Preterism does the same with the Rapture.

> But I would not have you to be ignorant, brethren, concerning them which are asleep, that ye sorrow not, even as others which have no hope. For if we believe that Jesus died and rose again, even so them also which sleep in Jesus will God bring with him. For this we say unto you by the word of the Lord, that we which are alive and remain unto the coming of the Lord shall not prevent them which are asleep. For the Lord himself shall descend from heaven with a shout, with the voice of the archangel, and with the trump of God: and the dead in Christ

shall rise first: Then we which are alive and remain shall be caught up together with them in the clouds, to meet the Lord in the air: and so shall we ever be with the Lord. Wherefore comfort one another with these words (1 Thess. 4:13-18).

Paul insists that the dead in Christ shall rise first, and then those who are still alive shall be caught up (raptured) to meet, and greet the coming Lord who is returning for the second time for all who believe. There is no escaping a literal, physical, bodily resurrection of the dead. This event cannot be spiritualized.

The Preterist have to insist on a secret, and silent Rapture in order to spiritualize this event and make the Rapture a historical reality. Their position is that nobody heard the Rapture, no one saw it, no one recorded it, but it happened spiritually. If the return of Christ did take place in the first century, it is the best kept secret in Church history.

Today, many Christians believe the Rapture of the Church, and a first resurrection takes place prior to a Great Tribulation. This is known as the Pretribulation Rapture Theory. In this Pretribulation Rapture scheme, Jesus will come near the earth for his saints, and then disappear with them into heaven, only to reappear seven years later for His final manifestation in glory. On this return flight, Jesus will rule the earth from Jerusalem for one thousand literal years.

These two stages, or two-phase Rapture, misses the imagery of 1 Thessalonians 4. The image is that of a returning hero who is greeted in his glory, and escorted back to the place to which he is coming. Jesus Christ is the King of kings who shall return the second time, and not in stages, or phases. But He shall return in glory, manifested with the shout of the archangel, the trump of God, the rising of the saints to greet Him, the resurrection of the dead, and His decent to earth. Which also said, Ye men of Galilee, why stand ye gazing up into heaven? this same Jesus, which is taken up from you into heaven, shall so come in like manner as ye have seen him go into heaven" (Acts 1:11). "So Christ was once offered to bear the sins of many; and unto them that look for him shall he appear the second time without sin unto salvation" (Heb. 9:28).

The return of Christ is reflected in the victorious return of a Roman military officer. The commanding Roman military general would place his camp, and all of his entourage, outside the gates of the city of Rome. A message would be sent to the Senate that he had returned. There would be great preparations made to receive the coming conquering hero. An arch of triumph would be built. Buildings and streets would be made clean and decorated. Garlands with a sweet aroma would be strewn to cover up any stench. At a prearranged time a signal would be made whereby the trumpets would sound announcing the hero. The armies of Rome would march in triumph into Rome. All the citizens of Rome were invited to come outside the city, join the triumphant army, and march back into the city so that they participated in the victory and in the triumph. When Jesus comes, He shall return with all the saints. He will continue to descend and meet with resurrected saints. What a future awaits Christians!

Chapter 13

Being Caught Up

In any discussion, it is important to define a term used in a technical sense, lest there be a misunderstanding. After 1830, a new word, "rapture," was introduced into the consciousness of the Church. Why this particular word has found so much popularity in the Church is curious, since it is from the Latin, and is not found in the Greek, or Hebrew.

From the Latin, "*rapiō*," the "catching up," comes the English word, "rapture." The English word is derived from the Vulgate, a Latin version of the Bible, authorized and used, by the Roman Catholic Church. The term is used in the translation of 1 Thessalonians 4:17.

Keeping in mind that how a word is used in the context of a sentence defines it meaning, it can be noted the word rapture could mean, a state, or experience of being carried away by overwhelming emotion. For example, "The people listened with rapture as the orchestra played Handel's *Messiah*." The meaning is that the people enjoyed a state, or experience of being carried away by overwhelming emotion.

The word rapture could refer to a personal, mystical experience, in which the spirit is exalted to a knowledge of divine things. "When I mediate, and try to feel the presence of God, my eyes close in rapture." In this usage of the word, the soul is exalted to a knowledge of divine things.

When the word is used as a proper noun by Dispensationalist, the Rapture refers to something specific.

In the eighteenth century, John Nelson Darby made popular the concept of a "secret rapture" whereby Christ would come, without warning, and take the Church, by force, to heaven, leaving the unbelieving world behind, to face the antichrist, seven years of tribulation, and the wrath of God. (Eerdmans Dictionary of the Bible) The Rapture is to precede the Lord's Second Advent by seven years.

It is true that, "those of varying millennial views about end time events all hold firmly to the biblical truth of such a rapture. However, it is within the premillennial view that the teaching of a rapture finds major emphasis." (Holman Bible Dictionary)

There is No Secret Coming in Scripture

The New Testament does not even use the word "secret" with reference to the coming of Christ except in one passage and that is to warn against those who will teach falsely and declare the Lord has come again and is in His secret chamber. Jesus said, "Believe them not!" (Matt. 24:26).

Jesus has promised to return the second time (Heb. 9:28) as a thief in the night (Matt. 24:43; Luke. 12:39; 1 Thess. 5:2; 2 Pet. 3:10; Rev. 3:3, 16:15) which means the Lord will come again at an unexpected time. The hour and date of His return is unknown to all but the Father.

The scriptural passages that explicitly uses the phrase "thief in the night" do so to indicate the day of the Lord will be unexpected and to warn believers to be alert and to be found faithful in prayer.

Those who are sober and alert need never fear the return of Christ. In 1 Thessalonians 5:4 the promise is given to the Church that Jesus will *not* come as a thief to them. When the Lord appears, the Church will see Him return in the clouds and will understand and will rise to welcome Him with love. All others will be surprised. How is this possible? Consider.

A thief who is being watched can do something as long as deception is used. For example. Imagine a moving van stopping in front of the house of a neighbor that is not well known. Nothing is really thought of the matter until the neighbor returns, walks into the house and starts to scream, "Someone stole all my furniture!" Others saw all the men, the van, and the belongings in the house but it did not dawn on anyone what the thieves were up to. That is the way it will be when the Lord returns. Every eye will see Him, but many will not know or understand who He is or what He is up to until it's too late. Jesus will come back to earth by way of the air (Acts 1) but only the Church will understand so that the Day of the Lord does not take them as a thief.

The secret pretribulation rapture is so secret that the Church never heard of it for 1,830 years.

Chapter 14

The Rapture Theory and Harpazō

"Beloved, when I gave all diligence to write unto you of the common salvation, it was needful for me to write unto you, and exhort you that ye should earnestly contend for the faith which was once delivered unto the saints" (Jude 3).

Those who believe in Dispensational Theology appeal to the Greek word *harpazō* in defense of their understanding of the Rapture, which is generally understood in Dispensationalism as that particular event when the Church is caught away, or raptured, from earth, in order for a seven-year period of tribulation to begin.

It is believed by many that the Church is going to escape a special great tribulational period, though there is no verse in the Bible which uses the word *thlipsis*, tribulation, to support this idea. Jesus said, "These things I have spoken unto you, that in me ye might have peace. In the world ye shall have tribulation: but be of good cheer; I have overcome the world" (John 16:33). Paul taught that, "we must through much tribulation enter into the kingdom of God."

The great tribulation that Israel was prophesied to endure in Matthew 24, Mark 13, and Luke 21, is today a historical reality, for Jesus said that everything which He predicted during the Olivet Discourse would happen within the generation to which He spoke. "Verily I say unto you, This generation shall not pass, till all these things be fulfilled" (Matt. 24:34). History confirms that what Christ predicted in A.D. 30, occurred between A.D. 66–70 with the fall of Jerusalem. Jesus was a Priest, a King, and a Prophet. The sign of a prophet was to be correct. All that Jesus said would happen, did happen.

A good place to begin the consideration of the position of Dispensational Theology on this matter is with a definition. Strong's Definition of *harpazō*: verb, to seize (in various applications): AV, catch (away, up), pluck, pull, take (by force).

Notice that the word *harpazō*, as used in the NT, is a verb, not a noun. Also, there is no definite article in any biblical verse which uses *harpazō*. The following Scriptures (*Septuagint*, LXX) contain the word *harpazō*.

> And from the days of John the Baptist until now the kingdom of heaven suffereth violence, and the violent take [*harpazō*] it by force [*harpazō*] (Matt. 11:12).
>
> When any one heareth the word of the kingdom, and understandeth it not, then cometh the wicked one, and catcheth away [*harpazō*] that which was sown in his

heart. This is he which received seed by the way side (Matt. 13:19).

When Jesus therefore perceived that they would come and take [*harpazō*] him by force [*harpazō*], to make him a king, he departed again into a mountain himself alone (John 6:15).

But he that is an hireling, and not the shepherd, whose own the sheep are not, seeth the wolf coming, and leaveth the sheep, and fleeth: and the wolf catcheth [*harpazō*] them, and scattereth the sheep (John 10:12).

And I give to them eternal life; and they shall never perish, neither shall any man pluck [*harpazō*] them out of my hand (John 10:28).

My Father, which gave them me, is greater than all; and no man is able to pluck [*harpazō*] them out of my Father's hand (John 10:29).

And when they were come up out of the water, the Spirit of the Lord caught away [*harpazō*] Philip, that the eunuch saw him no more: and he went on his way rejoicing (Acts 8:39).

And when there arose a great dissension, the chief captain, fearing lest Paul should have been pulled in pieces of them, commanded the soldiers to go down, and to take [*harpazō*] him by force [*harpazō*] from among them, and to bring him into the castle (Acts 23:10).

I knew a man in Christ above fourteen years ago, (whether in the body, I cannot tell; or whether out of the body, I cannot tell: God knoweth;) such an one caught up [*harpazō*] to the third heaven (2 Cor. 12:2).

How that he was caught up [*harpazō*] into paradise, and heard unspeakable words, which it is not lawful for a man to utter (2 Cor. 12:4).

Then we which are alive and remain shall be caught up [*harpazō*] together with them in the clouds, to meet the Lord in the air: and so shall we ever be with the Lord (1 Thess. 4:17).

And others save with fear, pulling [*harpazō*] them out of the fire; hating even the garment spotted by the flesh (Jude 1:23).

And she brought forth a man child, who was to rule all nations with a rod of iron: and her child was caught up [*harpazō*] to God, and to his throne (Rev. 12:5).

In none of these verses does the word *harpazō* speak of going away from earth for seven years, only to return with Christ again.

Dispensationalists like to speak of Christ coming for His Church in the Rapture, and then returning with His Church at the Second Advent proper. The Christian Church has consistently believed that at the Second Advent of Jesus, believers shall be caught up to greet the descending Christ who has promised to come again, the second time, for all who believe. Christ shall return in the same manner in which He ascended into heaven following His resurrection.

> Which also said, Ye men of Galilee, why stand ye gazing up into heaven? this same Jesus, which is taken up from you into heaven, shall so come in like manner as ye have seen him go into heaven (Acts 1:11).

> So, Christ was once offered to bear the sins of many; and unto them that look for him shall he appear the second time without sin unto salvation (Heb. 9:28).

What the historic Christian Church has never officially believed, or stated, in any Creed, in any Confession of Faith, or discussed in any ecumenical council, is the idea of a "rapture" being a separate event from the return of Jesus according to promise. In no biblical passage where *harpazō* is used is there the idea of Christians disappearing from earth for seven years only to return again.

The popular Dispensational teaching of the Rapture is the figment of human imagination, and not a clear exegesis of Scripture. Nor does the Rapture find any support in the Church Fathers.

Christians, who want to embrace the simplicity of Scripture, and a historic faith, should be concerned, because the Rapture theory transforms every other facet of Christian theology. It changes what the Church has taught historically about salvation, Israel, the Moral Law, and the Church.

Chapter 15

The London Baptist Confession of Faith of 1689

After 1830 a new word was introduced into the consciousness of the Church. That word is the word *rapture*. Why this particular word has found so much popularity in the Church is curious, since it is a Latin word, and is not found in the original Greek or Hebrew text of sacred Scripture. It is possible that if the Church had stayed with the Greek New Testament and the word *harpazō* meaning, "caught up," there might not be the controversy concerning the second coming of Christ that has developed.

It is instructive to remember that none of the Creeds of Christendom throughout Church history, and none of the Church Councils ever addressed the concept of the Rapture as it is taught today, namely, a separate event from the Second Coming. God's people have not been ignorant of God's Word for more than 1,800 years. They simply contended for the historic faith of the Church and set aside novel ideas. Notice the Scripture references the Baptist Confessions of Faith are built upon. Notice there are no multiple comings of Christ, and there are no multiple resurrections of the dead, which belief in a Dispensational Rapture mandates.

The London Baptist Confession of Faith of 1689

CHAPTER 31: OF THE STATE OF MAN AFTER DEATH, AND OF THE RESURRECTION OF THE DEAD

PARAGRAPH 1. The bodies of men after death return to dust, and see corruption;[1] but their souls, which neither die nor sleep, having an immortal subsistence, immediately return to God who gave them.[2] The souls of the righteous being then made perfect in holiness, are received into paradise, where they are with Christ, and behold the face of God in light and glory, waiting for the full redemption of their bodies;[3] and the souls of the wicked are cast into hell; where they remain in torment and utter darkness, reserved to the judgment of the great day;[4] besides these two places, for souls separated from their bodies, the Scripture acknowledgeth none.

[1] Gen. 3:19; Acts 13:36
[2] Eccles. 12:7
[3] Luke 23:43; 2 Cor. 5:1, 6, 8; Phil. 1:23; Heb. 12:23
[4] Jude 6, 7; 1 Peter 3:19; Luke 16:23, 24

PARAGRAPH 2. At the last day, such of the saints as are found alive, shall not sleep, but be changed;[5] and all the dead shall be raised up with the selfsame bodies, and none other;[6] although with different qualities, which shall be united again to their souls forever.[7]

[5] 1 Cor. 15:51, 52; 1 Thess. 4:17
[6] Job 19:26, 27
[7] 1 Cor. 15:42, 43

PARAGRAPH 3. The bodies of the unjust shall, by the power of Christ, be raised to dishonour; the bodies of the just, by his Spirit, unto honour, and be made conformable to his own glorious body.[8]

[8] Acts 24:15; John 5:28, 29; Phil. 3:21

CHAPTER 32: OF THE LAST JUDGMENT

PARAGRAPH 1. God has appointed a day wherein he will judge the world in righteousness, by Jesus Christ;[1] to whom all power and judgment is given of the Father; in which day, not only the apostate angels shall be judged,[2] but likewise all persons that have lived upon the earth shall appear before the tribunal of Christ, to give an account of their thoughts, words, and deeds, and to receive according to what they have done in the body, whether good or evil.[3]

[1] Acts 17:31; John 5:22, 27
[2] 1 Cor. 6:3; Jude 6
[3] 2 Cor. 5:10; Eccles. 12:14; Matt. 12:36; Rom. 14:10, 12; Matt. 25:32–46

PARAGRAPH 2. The end of God's appointing this day, is for the manifestation of the glory of his mercy, in the eternal salvation of the elect; and of his justice, in the eternal damnation of the reprobate, who are wicked and disobedient;[4] for then shall the righteous go into everlasting life, and receive that fullness of joy and glory with everlasting rewards, in the presence of the Lord; but the wicked, who do not know God, and do not obey the gospel of Jesus Christ, shall be cast aside into everlasting torments,[5] and punished with everlasting destruction, from the presence of the Lord, and from the glory of his power.[6]

[4] Rom. 9:22, 23
[5] Matt. 25:21, 34; 2 Tim. 4:8
[6] Matt. 25:46; Mark 9:48; 2 Thess. 1:7–10

PARAGRAPH 3. As Christ would have us to be certainly persuaded that there shall be a day of judgment, both to deter all men from sin,[7] and for the greater consolation of the godly in their adversity,[8] so will he have the day unknown to men, that they may shake off all carnal security, and be always watchful, because they know not at what hour the Lord will come,[9] and may ever be prepared to say, Come Lord Jesus; come quickly.[10] Amen.

[7] 2 Cor. 5:10,11
[8] 2 Thess. 1:5–7
[9] Mark 13:35-37; Luke 12:35–40
[10] Rev. 22:20

The 2000 Baptist Faith & Message

X. LAST THINGS

God, in His own time and in His own way, will bring the world to its appropriate end. According to His promise, Jesus Christ will return personally and visibly in glory to the earth; the dead will be raised; and Christ will judge all men in righteousness. The unrighteous will be consigned to Hell, the place of everlasting punishment. The righteous in their resurrected and glorified bodies will receive their reward and will dwell forever in Heaven with the Lord.

Isa. 2:4; 11:9; Matt. 16:27; 18:8–9; 19:28; 24:27, 30, 36, 44; 25:31–46; 26:64; Mark 8:38; 9:43–48; Luke 12:40,48; 16:19–26; 17:22–37; 21:27–28; John 14:1–3; Acts 1:11; 17:31; Rom. 14:10; 1 Cor. 4:5; 15:24–28, 35–58; 2 Cor. 5:10; Phil. 3:20–21; Col. 1:5; 3:4; 1 Thess. 4:14–18; 5:1ff.; 2 Thess. 1:7ff.; 2; 1 Tim. 6:14; 2 Tim. 4:1,8; Titus 2:13; Heb. 9:27–28; Jas. 5:8; 2 Pet. 3:7ff.

Chapter 16

Is the Rapture a Coming of Christ, or Not?

"For the Lord himself shall descend from heaven with a shout, with the voice of the archangel, and with the trump of God: and the dead in Christ shall rise first: Then we which are alive and remain shall be caught up together with them in the clouds, to meet the Lord in the air: and so shall we ever be with the Lord. Wherefore comfort one another with these words" (1 Thess. 4:16–18).

"Which also said, Ye men of Galilee, why stand ye gazing up into heaven? this same Jesus, which is taken up from you into heaven, shall so come in like manner as ye have seen him go into heaven" (Acts 1:11).

"So, Christ was once offered to bear the sins of many; and unto them that look for him shall he appear the second time without sin unto salvation" (Heb. 9:28).

Question: Because "the System," known as Dispensationalism, teaches that Christ does not physically touch earth during the Rapture event, should the Rapture be considered a coming of Christ?

Question: Since Christ does not actually return to the ground, is that considered a coming?

At some point, a little prior to or soon after 1830, an exciting concept was introduced into the mainstream consciousness of the Church, first in England, and then in America. The leading proponent of this concept was John Nelson Darby.

The idea was presented, that prior to end time, a great period of trouble will come upon the earth, which is to last for seven years, Jesus will come, or return, to take the Church away, so that God's people do not have to go through the tribulational wrath to come.

Paul went through tribulation, as will every Christian who names the name of Christ. There is not a single verse in the Bible that teaches that the Church, or Christians, shall escape tribulation. Just the opposite is taught.

Jesus said, "These things I have spoken unto you, that in me ye might have peace. In the world ye shall have tribulation: but be of good cheer; I have overcome the world" (John 16:33).

Paul went about, "Confirming the souls of the disciples, and exhorting them to continue in the faith, and that we must through much tribulation enter into the kingdom of God" (Acts 14:22).

The theory of the Rapture itself, whereby Christians (the Church) disappear in order to avoid tribulation, is unbiblical. It is also unheard of in any of the twenty-one Church ecumenical councils, or any of the Church creeds, or Confessions of faith. It is not found in the Baptist Confession of Faith. Why this historical silence on such an important doctrine? Answer: because is not found in the Bible, but in the vain imaginations of Margret MacDonald, Edward Irving, John Nelson Darby, C. I Scofield, and others who have embraced the Rapture theory.

Eventually, this coming of Christ for the Church, was distinguished from Christ coming with His Church to establish His reign on earth that was to last 1,000 years.

In time, the coming of Christ for the Church, prior to a time of great tribulation, began to be called the Rapture.

The main passage appealed to for this teaching is 1 Thessalonians 4:16-18.

The leading Dispensational Teachers establishing The System, advocating a coming of Christ for the Church to remove it from tribulation, were unanimous in calling the event a "coming" of Christ. Dr. John Walvoord, former president of Dallas Theological Seminary was the leading voice of Dispensational thinking in the 20th century. Commenting on 1 Thessalonians 4:16-17 he notes:

> The Scriptures also seem to make it very clear that when Christ comes *for* His own He will take them to heaven where He has gone now to prepare a place for us in the Father's house (John 14:1-3). Thereafter on the earth, while the church is in glory, will take place the great climactic event of this age—the great tribulation, and the out-calling of a great many Jews and Gentiles even in that awful time who come to trust in Christ. There will be

many martyrs in this period. The climax will come when Christ *returns* in power and glory with the angels and with the church from heaven to set up His righteous kingdom on the earth (*The Thessalonian Epistles*, John Walvoord).

I have emphasized the words, "for," and "returns" because Dr. Walvoord slips in a third coming of Christ, despite knowing the limitation of Hebrews 9:28, which says Christ will only come "the second time" for all who believe.

Dr. Walvoord taught that the return of Christ was to be achieved in two distinct events, or one second coming in two "phases," or stages. The first "stage" would be the Rapture, and the second "stage" would be the Second Advent proper. Such language is absolutely nonsensical, but it is the standard language of Dispensationalism. It is silly to talk about two events, going in opposite directions, separated by seven years, as really being ONE event, in two stages, or phases.

In reality, the Dispensationalist's coming of Christ in the Rapture is actually a third coming, and people should understand that, be honest about it, and state it plainly.

Both the Bible, and the historical faith of the Church, have advocated a Second Coming of Christ. The second coming (or return) of Christ is contained as an article of faith in all the ancient creeds:

> He ascended into heaven. From thence He shall come to judge the living and the dead (Apostles' Creed).

He shall come again with glory to judge both the living and the dead (Nicene Creed).

From thence he shall come to judge the living and the dead, at whose coming all men must rise with their bodies and are to render an account of their deeds (Athanasian Creed).

When the Scriptures are opened, simply read, and nothing is read into them, there is nothing in 1 Thessalonians 4:16-17 about Christians leaving earth for seven years, only to return later.

There is nothing about Christians going into heaven, for any other reason, than to meet the coming King of kings and Lord of lords.

The conclusion is this: Those who teach the Rapture, teach that Christ is coming *for* His saints in the Rapture, and then He is coming *with* His saints at the Second Advent Proper, seven years later.

The Rapture has always been presented by the leading advocates of Dispensationalists as a coming of Christ. They use the term "return" of Christ, but it is understood that the Rapture is a coming of Christ. *Merriam-Webster* defines "coming" as "an act or instance of arriving."

Yes, the Rapture is considered a "coming" of Christ by those who teach it. The larger question is this: "Should the Rapture be taught?" I would say, "NO!" The history of the Church says, "NO!"

Jude 3, "Beloved, when I gave all diligence to write unto you of the common salvation, it was needful for me to write unto you, and exhort you that ye should earnestly contend for the faith which was once delivered unto the saints."

Many Christians disagree, believe in, and advocate the Rapture. What was once advanced as a novel idea, has taken root in the Church. In the end, every person has to be persuaded in their own mind, by being a Berean, and searching the Scriptures on this matter.

Chapter 17

What About Old Testament Rapture Types?

Enoch, Noah, Lot, Joseph, and Elijah are sometimes presented by Dispensational teachers as types of the Church being caught up before the tribulation period. Such "types" are selected in an arbitrary manner, and overlook all the Old Testament saints who were preserved through great tribulation. Ruth knew the tribulation of sorrow and suffering, and yet endure through it all. The three Jewish men in the fiery furnace of Nebuchadnezzar's went through tribulation, and were preserved. Daniel went through tribulation, but was preserved in the den of the lions. Jeremiah was preserved, despite being in much tribulation during the Babylonian captivity.

When Enoch was taken by God, there was no tribulation on the earth. His selection is ironic, because The System constantly refers to the signs of the time as evidence of some great tribulation period coming, while ignoring the Genocide against Christians that is currently taking place in the Middle East in this very hour.

Note also that Noah was not "raptured," but was delivered through the tribulation that came to the world. God preserved Noah through the Flood. Lot was not "raptured," but was taken outside the cities of destruction of Sodom and Gomorrah. Joseph, in the midst of the suffering of his people helped to provide for them. Elijah was taken to heaven, not in order to escape any coming tribulation period, but simply because his work was done, and the Lord chose to honor him in a very special way.

The teaching that Enoch is a type of the Church raptured, or translated prior to tribulation, is based on the presuppositional thought that the Bible teaches a Rapture according to The System called Dispensationalism. That is a false presupposition, for there is not a single verse in the Bible that teaches the Church is to be secretly, silently, removed from earth to go to heaven, only to return seven years later.

The System of Dispensationalism first presuppositions many ideas, and then goes to the Bible to find an example to fit the idea. That technique is called eisegesis, or reading into the Bible what is not there. A faithful interpretation of Scripture is based on exegesis, or reading out of a text what is stated.

Be faithful to the simplicity of God's word, and all shall be well. But, do not raise the hopes and dreams of Christians.

Raising False Expectations

One way this is done, as well meaning as it may be, is by speaking about the imminent, or, likely to occur at any moment, return of Christ. No one knows that. No one can say the return of Christ is likely to happen within an hour, a day, a month, a year, or a given generation. Historically, prior to 1830, the Church was more cautious, and taught the concept of an impending return of Jesus Christ, never losing faith in the blessed hope that Jesus would return the second time according to promise (Heb. 9:28).

Peter warns the Church not to despair because of the Lord's delay. "The Lord is not slack concerning his promise, as some men count slackness; but is longsuffering to us-ward, not willing that any should perish, but that all should come to repentance" (2 Pet. 3:9).

By speaking of an imminent return, and then pointing to current events, people can become careless, and fail to live soberly, and righteously as they should. They can be easily misled and mistaught. Many can be made merchandise of. The temptation arises to embrace foolishness, and speculation, reflected in the Millerite movement whereby people sold their possessions, or gave important items, away believing the world was coming to an end. Christians should have just patiently waited for the glorious appearance of our great God and Savior.

A Careful Exegesis of the Bible Must Take Place Within the Context of Scripture

Scriptural interpretation is not to be based upon pre-suppositional thoughts, for that is isogesis, meaning a reading into the text what one desires it to mean. Eisegesis inevitably leads to heresy, which is extreme error. The faithful student of the Bible is to rightly divide the Word of Truth. "Study to shew thyself approved unto God, a workman that needeth not to be ashamed, rightly dividing the word of truth" (2 Tim. 2:15).

Rightly dividing the Word of Truth does not mean to chop the Scriptures up into arbitrary periods of time in order to make a theological construct in which to pigeon hole favorite texts in order to teach favorite concepts.

Ministers are, "Not to invent a new gospel, but rightly to divide the gospel that is committed to their trust. To speak terror to those to whom terror belongs, comfort to whom comfort; to give everyone his portion in due season." So says the good Matthew Henry.

William Miller did not always use sound hermeneutical principles when studying the Bible, and he led multitudes into error, or worse. Mr. Miller brought shame, disillusionment, and disgrace to the Church of God. He did not mean to, but he did.

Apart from the Illuminating Work of the Holy Spirit, People can become Convinced and Confirmed in Their Error

In 1818 William Miller was convinced he had found the key to unlock the secret of the Second Advent of Christ. He continued in his studies until 1823 "to ensure the correctness of his interpretation," and became confirmed in error. There is a principle of divine judgment which can be summarized in this manner: "Those who will not change, will find they cannot change." "He that is unjust, let him be unjust still: and he which is filthy, let him be filthy still: and he that is righteous, let him be righteous still: and he that is holy, let him be holy still" (Rev. 22:11).

Beware of Using Current Events

When I was growing up in Dallas, Texas, I was taught as a child that no one can know the day or hour of the Lord's return, but we can know the generation. In other words, a time-period was established. Then the template was presented. A biblical generation is about 40 years. Since Israel was re-established as a nation in 1948, we can believe that Christ will return within a forty-year time period. Therefore, 1988 was to be the year of the Lord's return, and maybe even 1981, if you take away seven years for a tribulation period. To people growing up in the 50s, 60s, and 70s, it was exciting to believe that the 1980s would bring a countdown to Armageddon, and then the millennium. It was also wrong.

Chapter 18

Personal Concerns with Classical Dispensationalism and the Rapture

In addition to knowing the historical narrative regarding modern Premillennial Dispensationalism and its emphasis on the Rapture, and in addition to the lessons that can be learned from its failures, there are specific concerns to consider. The following are my own concerns with "The System," as I call it, for Classical Premillennial Dispensationalism is a System of Prophetic Understanding, finely tuned over many years, and constantly changing. "True truth", as the theologian and philosopher Francis Schaeffer would say, does not change (Jude 3).

The System employs incomprehensible vocabulary. Dispensational writers often speak of the Second Coming of Christ in two Phases. Phase One: The Rapture. Phase Two: The Second Advent Proper. People do not normally talk about going somewhere in two stages, separated by a seven-year period of time, with activity going in opposite directions, and calling everything one event. That is nonsensical language.

The System Spawns an inordinate fascination with prophetic signs. Jesus said that "an evil and adulterous generation seeketh after a sign." "Then certain of the scribes and of the Pharisees answered, saying, Master, we would see a sign from thee. 39 But he answered and said unto them, An evil and adulterous generation seeketh after a sign; and there shall no sign be given to it, but the sign of the prophet Jonas" (Matt. 12:38). Surely, the generations from 1830 to the present must be among the most evil and adulterous generations in human history, for the fascination with signs of the time is endless. This speculation has created disillusionment and spawned several cults, including the Seventh Day Adventist and the Jehovah Witnesses.

The System has a misplaced emphasis concerning the Antichrist. While lip service is given to looking for "The Blessed Hope," it seems that much attention, by prophetic pundits and enthusiasts, is really focused on discovering the Antichrist. I remember as a young person growing up in a strong dispensational Church in Dallas, Texas, the excitement generated in the Church with the pronouncement by the Catholic prophetesses Jean Dixon (1904–1997), that the Antichrist had been born. Jean Dixon foresaw a young man arising out of Egypt to rule the world in a vision she had February 5, 1962. She wrote,

> A child born somewhere in the Middle East shortly before 7:00 A.M. (EST) on February 5, 1962 will revolutionize the world. Before the close of this century, he will bring together all mankind in one all-embracing faith. This will be the foundation of a new Christianity, with every sect and creed united through this man who will walk among the people to spread the wisdom of the almighty powers.

Of course, Jean Dixon was wrong, but maybe, not by much. Some people believe the Antichrist was actually born on August 4, 1961 in Hawaii!

The System diminishes the importance of the Holy Spirit. There is the teaching that when the alleged rapture takes place, the Holy Spirit is removed from the earth in as far as He indwells Christians, but then, there will be a great revival that takes place during the alleged seven-year Great Tribulation period.

The System promotes false prophets. If a false prophet is someone who speaks in the name of the Lord, but whose predictions fail, then many preachers, teachers, and authors have much to fear. The list of those who have made predictions in the name of the Lord is long and shameful.

> But the prophet, which shall presume to speak a word in my name, which I have not commanded him to speak, or that shall speak in the name of other gods, even that prophet shall die. And if thou say in thine heart, How shall we know the word which the Lord hath not spoken? When a prophet speaketh in the name of the Lord, if the

thing follows not, nor come to pass, that is the thing which the Lord hath not spoken, but the prophet hath spoken it presumptuously: thou shalt not be afraid of him" (Deut. 18:20–22).

I want to be charitable, and careful. It is possible for a Bible teacher to be in error without being charged with being a false prophet. A Christian can have a good heart, but bad theology. Nevertheless, care must be taken. There is real danger in becoming a false prophet by speaking in the name of the Lord about events which will not come to pay. There are many false prophets in the world today.

The System is based on a presuppositional thought that God has two people, two plans, two programs, one is earthly, one is heavenly, and never the two shall meet. One is called Israel, the other is called the Church. An appeal for this dramatic distinction is made to 1 Corinthians 10:32. "Give none offence, neither to the Jews, nor to the Gentiles, nor to the Church of God." But what if God has one plan, one people, one program, one destiny, and the two meets in Christ.

> There is neither Jew nor Greek, there is neither bond nor free, there is neither male nor female: for ye are all one in Christ Jesus (Gal. 3:28).

> Know ye therefore that they which are of faith, the same are the children of Abraham. 8 And the scripture, foreseeing that God would justify the heathen through faith,

preached before the gospel unto Abraham, saying, In thee shall all nations be blessed (Gal. 3:7).

Concerning the Jews, The System condemns millions to death, and even encourages a subtle form of anti-Semitism. Consider the evidence. Depending upon which prophetic expert is read, two out of three Jews of some generation, perhaps ours, is doomed to liquidation. It is inevitable. Why then, do some strongly Dispensational organizations raise money to send Jewish people to live in Israel believing it might hasten the Rapture, and thus their annihilation? Specifically, John Hagee's ministry has given millions of dollars to bring the Jewish exiles of the world home to Israel, all the while believing multitudes will die in a future holocaust.

A more biblical, and historical, response to this type of thinking is, "Jews do not have to die." Judgment and calamity can be avoided by gospel repentance.

One of the great truths of Scripture is that Jesus Christ is prophet, priest, and king. The prophetic and priestly offices of Jesus are more readily conceded, but there is still a discussion concerning the kingly office of Christ by many Christians. Two distinct schools of thought prevail. There is a belief that the kingly office of Jesus is still to be held in the future. Many years ago I was sitting in a barbershop in Rogers, Arkansas. The owner was a firm believer in the Dispensational, millennium reign of Christ. He was convinced that one day in the future Jesus Christ would be king and rule the nations of the earth. Speaking to another man in the shop, the owner called out his name and said, "Do you think Jesus is a king. I don't. He is not my king. He is my Savior.

He is a prophet and priest. Someday He will be king, but not now." I wanted to ask, "Then who is your king? Who are you subject to? Who is your Master?"

The barber was not alone in his theological position. The idea of a future one thousand years reign of Christ, ruling in Jerusalem, from the restored throne of David, in a restored Temple, with restored animal sacrifices, is a fascinating concept that obscures the spiritual reality that belongs to the Church.

The biblical alternative to Jesus someday becoming a sovereign king, is that Jesus is even now King of all kings and Lord of all lords. He is even now exercising royal sovereignty. The evidence is set forth beginning in the gospels.

Evangelistic efforts are undermined. Imagine witnessing to someone and saying, "Did you know that we are living in the final days of human history. It is true. The world is about to end. The Antichrist has been born. There is no hope. And if that is not bad enough, I am a member of an apostate organization called the Church, which, technically, is in the Laodicea age. Uh, would you like to go to Sunday school with me this weekend?" A message of doom, self-loathing, and pessimism, is not a promising evangelistic message.

The System has some unique techniques to advance its teaching. One technique has been noted to combine two events separated by time, direction, and purpose, and make them one. In this way the Rapture and seven years later the Second Advent, can both be called the Second Advent, Phase I and Phase II.

Another unique technique of Dispensational Theology in association with understanding the fulfillment of prophecy, is to declare that ancient nations must reemerge. "And, of course, what we have seen is the reemergence of the nations of the ancient East and they have become the important nations, largely through the energy crisis, which has come upon us in the last few decades" (S. Lewis Johnson, 1979).

In order to make The System's teaching work, Dispensational teachers take a modern-day map, overlay it on top of Scriptural texts, and declare prophecy to be fulfilled now, instead of allowing prophecy to have been fulfilled according to promise historically with the biblical names of the nations. It is a clever technique—but it is wrong.

Iran is not Babylon. All that remains of the original ancient famed city of Babylon today is a large mound, or tell, of broken mud-brick buildings, and debris in the fertile Mesopotamian plain between the Tigris and Euphrates rivers. It is located 53 miles south of Bagdad. Greece is not the Greek Empire of Alexander the Great. Italy is not even a shadow of the Roman Empire. But the Church is the kingdom of heaven which fills the earth.

The System is not rooted in the historic faith of the Church. This is confirmed in part by reading the Creeds of Christendom, specifically the Apostles' Creed, the Nicene Creed, and the Athanasian Creed. What is within the historic faith, and all the Creeds of Christendom is that, "Christ shall come again with glory to judge both the quick and the dead, whose kingdom shall have no end" (Nicene Creed).

SOLI DEO GLORIA.

www.ingramcontent.com/pod-product-compliance
Lightning Source LLC
Chambersburg PA
CBHW061948070426
42450CB00007BA/1087